THE ROMAN FORTS OF THE SAXON SHORE

ELEK ARCHAEOLOGY AND ANTHROPOLOGY
General Editor: J. V. S. Megaw
Professor of Archaeology in the University of Leicester

Already published

The Environment of Early Man in the British Isles
John G. Evans

Science and Society in Prehistoric Britain
Euan W. MacKie

Greek Architects at Work
J. J. Coulton

Parthian Art
Malcolm A. R. Colledge

Industrial Archaeology in the British Isles
John Butt and Ian Donnachie

The Roman Forts of the Saxon Shore

Stephen Johnson

Paul Elek   London

First published in Great Britain in 1976 by
Elek Books Ltd
54–58 Caledonian Road, London N1 9RN

Second edition 1979

ISBN 0 236 40165 3

Printed in Great Britain at
The Camelot Press Ltd, Southampton

CONTENTS

FIGURES

ACKNOWLEDGEMENTS

In presenting a work of this nature, one cannot avoid drawing to a very large extent on the conclusions of scholars and excavators who have worked and are still working in the same field. For information about particular sites I am indebted to Chris Green and the Norfolk Archaeological Unit (on Brancaster), to Miss Barbara Green for free access to her father's notes and finds from his campaigns of excavations at Burgh Castle, and to Professor Barry Cunliffe for allowing me to read his report on the late Roman period at Portchester Castle well in advance of publication. To these and to all other excavators who have unearthed or are still unearthing new information about the Saxon Shore and its forts I owe a great debt of gratitude.

For the use of illustrative material I gratefully acknowledge permission from the following individuals and institutions: Professor J. Mertens and the Institut Royal du Patrimonie Artistique, Brussels (Fig. 3); the Photographic Library of the Department of the Environment (Figs. 6, 28, 37 and 68); Mr R. P. Wright and the Clarendon Press, Oxford (Fig. 9); the Ashmolean Museum, Oxford (Figs. 14–18); the Trustees of the British Museum (Fig. 19); the Trustees of the Victoria County History (Fig. 24); Mr Derek Edwards and the Norfolk Archaeological Unit (Fig. 21); the Royal Archaeological Institute (Figs. 26 and 83); the Society of Antiquaries for plans and drawings on which Figs. 30, 38, 55, 56, 61, 62, 74 and 82 are based; the Director General of the Ordnance Survey for the map on which Fig. 32 is based; the Bodleian Library, Oxford (Figs. 39, 41 and 42); and Professor Barry Cunliffe and Mike Rouillard (who took the photograph) for Fig. 35.

I am also grateful to the number of people who have helped in various ways to prepare this book for publication, foremost among whom is Professor Sheppard Frere, who throughout offered much helpful criticism and many welcome suggestions for improving the presentation.

The publication of a second edition of this work has made it possible for me to emend one or two points from the first edition, and to bring some of the descriptions of the various sites a little further up-to-date. The basic argument of the book, however, remains largely unaltered.

S. J.
November 1978

INTRODUCTION

The coastline was such that from the tops of the cliffs which bordered the sea
weapons could be hurled down on the shore below. This was in no way a suitable
place to attempt a landing. . . .

These first impressions of the coastline of Britain were recorded by Caesar in
55 B.C. Deterred by the menacing aspect of the cliffs at the south-eastern tip of
the British coastline, he sought and found a more suitable beach elsewhere to
act as the bridgehead for his attempt at invasion. Though his is the first record
of what an invader thought of the approach to Britain, Caesar was by no
means the first nor the last to try to gain a foothold on the island. The southern
and eastern shores are festooned with the remains of fortresses, castles, towers
and gun-emplacements intended to withstand invasion by hosts of different
enemies at all periods of Britain's history.

Like Caesar, some of these invaders were not deterred by the hostility of the
coastline. Among these were Saxon raiders and settlers: cruel, merciless
plunderers who attacked this fringe of the Roman empire in its last days and
joined in the concerted assault of Germanic tribes which eventually brought
the Roman empire to its knees. The Saxons were expert sailors and quicksilver
pirates, foes who struck fear into the hearts of civilized Romans and menaced
the peace and security of the Roman north.

Round Britain's southern and eastern coasts there still stand prominent
remains of the Roman forts which were built to withstand these raiders,
forerunners of many a similar series of heavily guarded posts protecting the
island's life. Some lie now completely buried; jagged fragments of walls of
others, still massive, once magnificent, point to the skies. All are eloquent
testimony to the power of Rome which built this frontier and maintained it
for more than a century against ever-increasing pressure.

These are the forts of the Saxon Shore: forts built in the third and fourth
centuries A.D. to defend Britain in a region which was now under surprise
attack. But despite the unexpectedness of the Saxon attacks, Roman tactical
genius developed an answering stratagem which fully exploited natural
resources of topography, while affording to both British and Continental
Channel shores as complete protection as could be against the suddenness and
unpredictability of the Saxon raids.

This book is an attempt to describe the workings of this system in full; to fill
in the backcloth against which the defensive scheme was first constructed; to
describe the forts as they are known today and to clothe them with something

of their Roman life and purpose; and finally to trace the later development of tactics to meet later exigencies. Nor is this study confined to Britain. The Saxon Shore forts were not merely concerned with the protection of Britain: they formed a Roman frontier, guarding the north-eastern reaches of the empire, including parts of northern Gaul. The defence of these areas and of Britain went hand in hand.

There are still many problems associated with the Saxon Shore, not least concerning its nature and origin. In offering a new, overall concept to the study of the Saxon Shore as a frontier line, it is hoped that the book will stimulate reconsideration of the difficulties of this neglected corner of the Roman defensive system, while at the same time providing a model for the study of other frontiers within the empire.

1 THE SETTING

The years at the end of the third century A.D. were a time of crisis throughout the Roman empire and especially so for the provinces of the north and west. Within all too recent memory, disasters had struck deep into the lives of the provincial citizens of Gaul and Britain. For more than a century, the frontiers of the empire had been static, and, if they were not peaceful all the time, at least they provided a solid defence against the unruliness of the barbarian outside. By degrees, during the course of the third century, this confidence was being worn away by repeated pressures from outside which from time to time resulted in a breach of the frontier and consequent damage to the undefended towns and cities of the interior parts of the provinces.

Invasion from the barbarian tribes was the most important threat which hung over the western empire at this time. In its wake it brought other disturbing results: military instability, civilian unrest, and perhaps even a loss of confidence in the Roman coinage. Within the Roman army itself, several separatist movements are known to have started at this period, when one or another group of troops supported their particular army commander as a rival imperial candidate to challenge the power of the emperor. Emperors themselves were as often as not appointed by acclaim of their armies and often frontier lines were stripped of men to add military weight to the imperial claims of a would-be emperor, laying the frontier and the civilian parts of the province open to barbarians.

Civilian unrest was most common in the form of uprisings by *Bagaudae*—a term used by contemporary historians and not now fully understood. They were probably in origin rough border countrymen and settlers, uprooted from their homes at the fringes of the empire because of the threat of invasion from without. Such men carried on a kind of guerrilla warfare, no doubt living on what they could steal in their raids. At the same time, monetary inflation was out of hand, possibly as a result of the unsettled times.

All over the empire, but especially in the Gallic provinces, there were setbacks and breaches of frontier security. New forts had to be built in an effort to stem the tide of invasion. In the decade 250–60, a large tract of territory opposite Mainz which had formed part of the Roman empire for about a century and a half was abandoned. Rome from now on was to have no claim on the area east of the Rhine: whole towns, walled and defended in Roman style, lying in this flat and fertile plain, were left to decay, and the task of rebuilding and strengthening old fort-sites along the bank of the Rhine where the army had not been stationed for over two centuries was begun.[1]

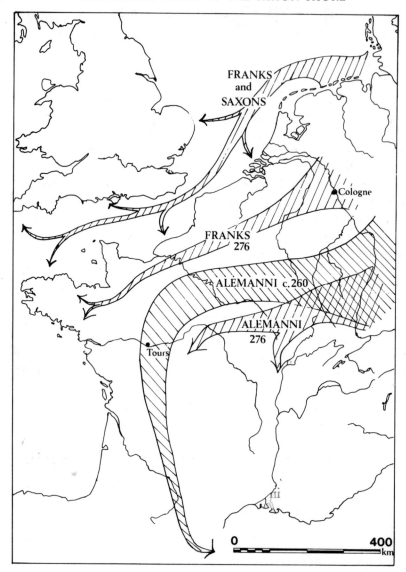

Fig. 1 Map of Gaul and Britain showing the main invasions
of the third century.

The episode of the usurpation of Postumus was the occasion of one of the
two most serious raids by German tribes in the latter part of the century (Fig.
1). The legitimate emperor, Gallienus, after a series of campaigns in Gaul, was
called away by further trouble in the east and had to leave his son, then still a
teenager, at Cologne to act as regent of the western frontier line. Gallienus left

in 258: by the next year, the army of the Rhine was in revolt, proclaiming their general Postumus as rival emperor. The young Caesar Saloninus in Cologne was assassinated. It seems likely that, taking advantage of this diversion, the Alemanni, one of a series of German tribes living in the neighbourhood of the frontier, crossed the Rhine into Roman territory and swept in a broad line through Gaul, possibly even reaching Spain.[2] Here, one historical source records that they commandeered ships and sailed for Africa.[3] Be that as it may, the invasion caused considerable disruption, and one of the first tasks undertaken by Postumus as the leader of the 'Gallic empire' was to make sure that the frontier defences were not again so easily breached. It may even have been this episode which led to the abandonment of the Roman territory east of the Rhine, compelling the Roman authorities to fall back on the river frontier, which was both easily visible and more easily defensible.

The Gallic separatist empire outlasted Postumus, and did not capitulate until 273, when his successor, Tetricus, surrendered to the legitimate Roman emperor, Aurelian, himself a successor of Gallienus. Aurelian was a strong military emperor, and probably was responsible for a number of defensive schemes which were instituted for Gaul. Unfortunately, he had little time to carry them out, for he was assassinated in 275, and within a short while a struggle developed between new rival candidates for imperial power, Florian and Probus, the former the Senate's choice, the latter the choice of the eastern armies. Once more, the Alemanni and other German tribes, taking advantage of the fact that Carus (another claimant to imperial power) had stripped the Rhine frontier of troops to support his claim, invaded, this time with more devastating effect. Probus won the battle for imperial supremacy, but his first and most pressing task was the restoration of the cities of Gaul. Some sixty or seventy were in barbarian hands, or had been thoroughly damaged in their raids of 276. Coin-hoards of this period, which probably show the broad lines followed by the German ʼvaders (Fig. 2), suggest that the raids were on three fronts: the Alemanni crossed the Rhine between Mainz and Basel, the Franks hit at the area of *Belgica Secunda*, while other tribes, possibly the Juthungi, may have joined in the attacks on Switzerland (*Maxima Sequanorum*) and Bavaria (*Raetia*).

The Roman response was in most cases immediate: not only was there strengthening of the frontier by Probus but also considerable rebuilding of Gallic towns and the provision of by now much needed defences. In Britain, too, some towns which had at best had earthwork defences by the beginning of the third century now found it necessary to have new walls which were usually inserted into the front of the earthen ramparts. The brunt of Continental invasion was not felt in the British provinces, but they did share one of the threatened areas—this was the maritime frontier, the sea-straits between Britain and Gaul.

For the Roman authorities, this coastline posed one of the greatest problems

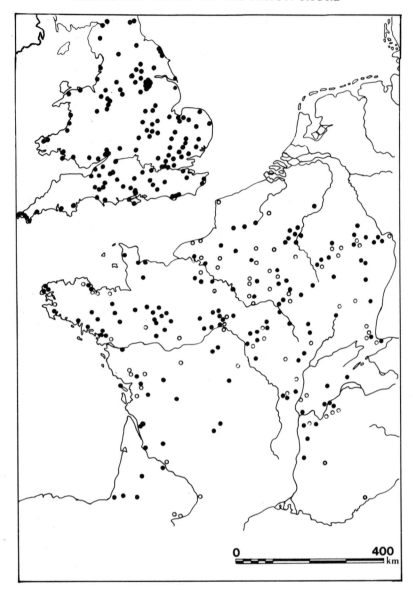

Fig. 2 Distribution map of coin-hoards of the period A.D. 270–85.
Unfilled circles indicate possible hoards.

of security. Britain was an important and prized part of the empire: her
mineral resources made her a rich source of the empire's wealth and her
security was therefore a matter of deep concern.[4] But not only was the Rhine
frontier breached by tribes who lived beyond it, but another tribe of seafarers
had established what was a virtual control of the sea-lanes between Britain

and the Continent. No longer was it safe to transfer goods or precious metal from Britain to the mainland of Europe: the Saxons were plunderers and would swoop at sea or on land to kill and rob. Contemporary sources graphically describe the Franks and Saxons, both seafaring tribes, infesting the seas and posing a dangerous double threat to the shores of Britain and of Gaul.[5]

It is important to stress that Britain was not the only area affected by these seaborne raids. There is an impressive series of coin-hoards from British coastal sites on the south and east which show the areas most threatened (Fig. 2).[6] Equally impressive is the series of hoards of the same period in the coastal areas, not only of northern Gaul, but also trailing down in a long line into the western provinces which line the coasts of Gaul, and even into districts of Spain.[7] Following this coastline, Saxons could surprise towns and communities deep within the empire: here there were no further frontier lines to cross and no permanent guards to alert. The danger of attack was real, not only in Britain, but also in formerly peaceful provinces of the western empire.

As this problem was not totally a British one, so its solution could not be confined to Britain alone. A series of new Roman forts was planned to strengthen harbour installations on both sides of the Channel. The harbours were fortified not only for the protection of the fleet and its personnel (which was now reorganized to cope more effectively with the danger) but also to provide safe cover for a mobile infantry or cavalry force intended to act as coastguards and combat corps to contest actual Saxon or Frankish pirate landings. Fortunately the Roman name for this system of defence has been preserved in a late Roman document called the *Notitia Dignitatum*. The defences were the forts of the *Litus Saxonicum*, the 'Saxon Shore'.

This name itself provides perhaps the first main problem. It was part of Roman policy at this period to settle groups of barbarian tribesmen inside the northern frontiers of the empire, usually with the double purpose of strengthening the failing agriculture of the regions worst hit by barbarian raiding and also of providing buffer states ready and able to supply auxiliary troops to supplement the regular Roman army, whenever the need arose.[8] Such tribesmen who were privileged enough to be allowed to move into the vacant areas inside the Roman empire would willingly join forces with the Roman frontier guards to maintain their position against encroachment from others less fortunate outside the empire. There is some slight evidence that as early as the end of the third century there may have been small pockets of Saxons settling in East Anglia, perhaps as part of this policy.[9] It might thus be supposed that the name 'Saxon Shore' grew up because this was an area of Saxon settlement over which the Romans held some control.[10]

The evidence for a date within the Roman period of settlement specifically by Saxons in the areas of eastern Britain and northern Gaul is very slight, but

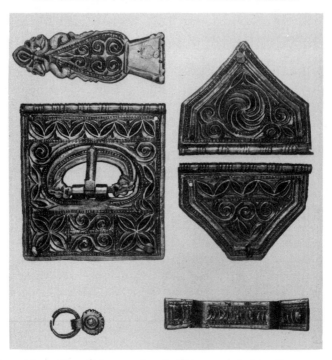

Fig. 3 The military metalwork of German style from Grave 3
of the cemetery at Oudenburg. Scale 1:2.

then traces of settlement are generally scanty and extremely hard to date with
any accuracy. That German troops from tribes outside the empire were used
as a kind of mercenary army in the later Roman period is suggested by
historical sources. Some trace of such *laeti* (the Roman term for these men)
may be seen in the distinctive style of military equipment—belt-plates,
buckles, and strap-ends—which was in use among the soldiery of the period.
That equipment like the set of belt-fittings found at Oudenburg (Fig. 3) is of
Germanic origin is not in doubt. Finds of this type of equipment are now
being recognized at many sites in Britain and on the Continent, but it is
difficult always to be certain from the style of a belt about the type of person
who used it. In Britain particularly, there is little reason to connect this style of
military equipment with settlers. Finds are still too slight to show any clear
picture of the disposition of *laeti* within Britain, and it is only on the
Continent, where some sites have produced impressive cemeteries containing
several good examples of this type of metalwork, that we can be certain that
there is some connection with these troops.[11]

The fact that a few examples of this type of metalwork have been found at
the Saxon Shore forts in Britain and the scattered literary references to the
deliberate settlement of Germanic tribes inside Britain[12] are insufficient to

prove that the Saxon Shore was so named because there were Saxons there. There is, of course, a strong likelihood that East Anglia was one of the first areas of Britain to be settled by Saxons, but there is no evidence that they were also present on the south coast within the Roman period. Gaul presents a parallel picture: literary testimonies relate that there were two main areas of Saxon settlement in Gaul, the Boulonnais and the Bessin.[13] Even in these known areas, however, there is at present no evidence for Saxon arrival as settlers until the later years of the fifth century. As we shall see, the Roman version of the 'Saxon Shore' extends not only through East Anglia and the south coast of Britain, but also into a broad sweep of the Gallic coastal territory.

Another class of material which has been thought to be of significance in assessing the scale of Saxon presence in the coastal areas of the south and east is the type of pottery known as 'Romano-Saxon'.[14] This type of pottery was made in Roman fabric and fashion (on a potter's wheel) but in many examples bears a style of ornamentation or shape which aligns it with later Saxon decoration and forms of pottery, and sets it apart from the main-stream of Romano-British pottery manufacture. The main problem posed by the discovery of this type of pottery, decorated with bosses, triangles of impressed dimples, slashed strokes, and the like, is to assess how far these decorative fashions reflect the presence of the Saxons with whom such styles are traditionally associated. Not least of the difficulties is the dating of such pottery forms, for pottery of this type, with few exceptions, has not yet been discovered in closely datable contexts. One of these exceptions is a find in

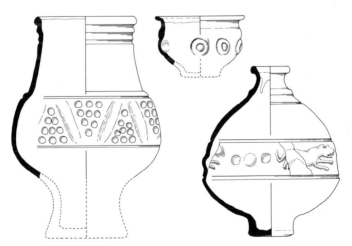

Fig. 4 Pottery of Romano-Saxon type from Burgh Castle.
The triangular formations of dimples are a typical
Saxon style. Scale 1:4.

which a jar bearing 'Romano-Saxon' decoration was used as a container for a hoard dating to A.D. 350–2.

If 'Romano-Saxon' pottery was current as early as this—and most of the site finds would suggest a date throughout the second half of the fourth century as normal—then there are two particular difficulties. One is that if this pottery is thought to be of late Roman fabric with Saxon decoration, there is little evidence that 'Saxon' styles of pottery of the period 350–400 had already started making use of these features which were to be so distinctive within its later development from 450–600 and beyond. The second difficulty is to envisage that an area of Britain could be so comprehensively settled by Saxons at this early date as to produce this distinctive type of pottery. Finds of examples of the style are beginning to show that it was fairly widespread, and it is also known from Continental sites.[15] A style of pottery with dimples and bosses ran in an undercurrent of local British style and tradition throughout the whole of the Roman occupation of Britain. 'Romano-Saxon' pottery, however, seems to be neither a continuation nor a culmination of this style: it has all the appearance of being made by competent Romano-British potters, perhaps from a relatively localized group of kilns. Its presence alone can scarcely be used to argue the advent of Saxon settlers in the period A.D. 350–400.

All in all, the more natural interpretation of the term 'Saxon Shore' is that it refers to an area of the coastline of Gaul and Britain which was under attack from Saxon raiders who had begun seriously to menace it at the end of the third century, if not before. Such raiding would be of a spasmodic nature—the Saxons were hit-and-run enemies who gained their major successes by surprise.[16] It is rare, if not unique, within the Roman empire to find a Roman frontier which was called by the name of its attackers. But tribal movements behind the inland river frontiers of Europe seem to have been relatively common, and there was therefore no other stretch of frontier within the Roman world which was so consistently under attack from the same direction and by the same single tribe.

The date at which the defensive area was christened the Saxon Shore cannot be closely defined. The earlier it was introduced, the more likely it is that the name was gained by Saxon attack rather than settlement. The first mention of Saxons in the coastal areas refers to the late third century: by the date that the *Notitia Dignitatum* was written down (commonly assumed to have been the latest years of the fourth century) the name was current and had been in use for some time. The Saxon threat, then, is recorded as becoming acute at the period when other parts of the empire were also under comparable pressure. The name probably occurs relatively soon after this date.

The new system of Saxon Shore forts was not a sudden phenomenon. The defence of the southern and eastern coasts of Britain had been a matter of priority for the Roman forces since the earliest years of the Roman occupation of Britain. The Channel formed the all-important link between Britain and the Continental supply routes—in particular Boulogne and the Rhine mouth, by far the most important Roman trading area. To protect Britain and the Channel routes to it, the British fleet, the *Classis Britannica*, was stationed at Boulogne and Dover. At the height of imperial power, this fleet protected the ungarrisoned wealthier parts of the province in southern and eastern Britain and this role became increasingly important as threats of piracy and raids from the Saxons became more and more real.

Several harbours and store bases in Britain are known to date from the period of invasion under Claudius, when the strategic link between fleet and legions must have been at its strongest. A newly discovered ditch of the Claudian period at Reculver adds a possible second early base to that already known and partially excavated at Richborough. Further bases no doubt await discovery in Kent. Supply ports which have been identified or suggested for the invasion period itself and for the following phase when the armies were still in need of seaborne supplies are at Fishbourne, Hamworthy and Topsham in the south and west, and at Fingringhoe in Essex.[17] Other coastal sites in Essex, notably those at the mouths of estuaries leading to Colchester, have produced finds of the Claudian period, but there is no definite evidence to link any of them with bases specifically for the fleet which brought the troops to Britain or supported the invasion.

In the early years after the conquest, Richborough appears to have been the most important of the British bases, for a large series of store-houses and granaries were built on the site. At Dover, too, there is evidence of use of the site in the first century; but it appears that the eventual eclipse of Richborough by Dover occurred only in the second century. A fort of second-century date has recently been discovered in the centre of the town of Dover. It was associated with many tiles (Fig. 5) stamped *CLBR* (for *Classis Britannica*) and vividly attests the presence of the British fleet at this base. The importance of Dover as a port in Roman times has long been evident from the impressive remains of the Roman lighthouse which stands on the hill dominating the town (Fig. 6). This is one of a pair which in Roman times guided shipping into the estuary of the Dour. No comparable site of similar date is known this side of the Channel and the fort at Dover may be the single base of the British fleet in Britain, with Boulogne performing a similar function on the Gallic side of the Channel (Fig. 7). It has generally been assumed, from the relative frequency of *CLBR* tiles, that Boulogne was the more important site. The new evidence from Dover may change our view of the relative importance of the two sites.

One of the most important involvements of the fleet in the second century was with the Wealden industries. Stamped tiles have been found there in

Fig. 5 Tile-stamps of the *Classis Britannica*. Scale 1 : 2

Fig. 6 *Left:* The 'Pharos' at Dover: a view of the second-century Roman lighthouse.

Fig. 7 *Right:* The Tour d'Odre at Boulogne, a Roman lighthouse originally similar to that at Dover, but now demolished.

contexts which suggest that the fleet was engaged in the production of iron and timber, both vital requisites of ship-building.[18] Tiles bearing the *CLBR* stamp are generally assumed to have been used only in buildings associated with the British fleet, and they are found in a second-century context at many places along the southern coastline of Britain between the Kent coast and the Isle of Wight. It has even been suggested that the commander of the fleet had a villa at Folkestone, where a large second-century villa built of tiles some of which bore the *CLBR* stamp was discovered in earliér years of this century.[19] The discovery of stamped tiles at sites deep into what is now Romney Marsh suggests that a great deal more of this area was navigable in Roman times, affording easier access to the Roman fleet. Much of the Weald will have been covered in forest and virtually intractable apart from along major road lines, of which few are at present known. That there are lost sites here is shown by an entry in Ptolemy's Geography, which locates a site called *Novus Portus*—Newport—in this part of the country. This may have been an until now unlocated base on the River *Novia*, which lay on the southern coast of Britain according to the author of the Ravenna Cosmography, a late fourth-century list of place-names throughout the Roman world.[20]

In *Gallia* and *Germania* there was also military activity on the coastline at a similar date (Figs. 8 and 10). There were sizeable fleet-bases at Boulogne and Étaples, where the estuary of the Canche housed a dockyard of comparable size and complexity to the one at Dover. Stamped tiles of the *Classis Britannica* are relatively common finds here and at Boulogne, but otherwise they are known only from Desvres. To the north-west along the coast was the sphere of influence of the *Classis Germanica* (the German fleet), whose tile-stamps *CGPF* (*Classis Germanica Pia Fidelis*) attest its presence in the second century at sites at the Rhine mouth in present-day Holland and at important sites along the Rhine itself in Germany.[21] Most of the forts along the lower stretch of the Rhine were also harbours; the site of the harbour itself is known at Zwammerdam and there were probably harbours also at Arentsburg and Vechten, where commanders of two legions set up altars to Neptune, the god of the sea.[22] Only two sites in the area of the Rhine mouth have produced tiles stamped by the German fleet. These are Wijk bij Duurstede and Leiden Roomburg, which is closely linked to the *Fossa Corbulonis* ('Corbulo's Ditch'), a Roman canal built in A.D. 47 to link the Helinium with the Old Rhine. Construction of this canal enabled a Roman fleet to reach the outer reaches of the river safely, and improved communications at the Rhine mouth.[23] Tile stamps of the *Classis Germanica*, though still rare finds on the Continent, seem to span the period between A.D. 86 and 170.

The majority of the information about the British fleet comes from the second century. In all, four names of commanders of the fleet have survived on inscriptions, and all are datable within the first half of the second century.

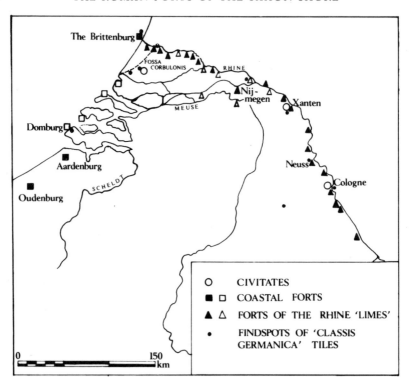

Fig. 8 Map showing second- and third-century military posts
in the Rhineland and Continental coastal areas.

Only one has a direct link with a southern coastal site. This is the altar set up by
Aufidius Pantera which was found reused and face down in the gateway of
the later fort at Lympne (Fig. 9). In the latter part of the first century, the fleet
was used primarily to back up the campaigns undertaken by Agricola in the
north, and possibly only later found its permanent station in the south-east. In
the second century, a number of coastal sites all round Britain may have
provided the harbours on which the *Classis Britannica* could be temporarily
based, or in which detachments of it could be permanently housed.

The latter part of the second century and the early part of the third were the
periods when Continental trade with Britain, especially from the Rhine, was
at a high peak. The Rhine mouth housed the harbours of Domburg,
Westerschouwen and Aardenburg, all of which were heavily in use in the
period from 180 to 220, as the coin-finds show. In addition, the sanctuary of
Nehalennia, a local goddess who seems to have been the special favourite of
sailors, was flourishing at the same time, to judge by the numbers of
dedications to her which have come from a site at Colijnsplaat, near
Domburg.[24]

Fig. 9 The altar set up by Aufidius Pantera at Lympne. The text and
translation runs: N] eptu [no/aram/L(ucius) Aufidius/
Pantera/praefect(us)/clas(sis) Brit(annicae), 'To Neptune, Lucius
Aufidius Pantera, praefect of the British Fleet, (set up this)
altar'. (RIB, 66; text, translation and figure reproduced by
courtesy of R. P. Wright and the Clarendon Press, Oxford.)

By the early third century, however, the peaceful picture was beginning to
change (Fig. 10). There is no evidence from historical writers that pressures
were being brought to bear on the coastal regions, but there are indications
from archaeological evidence that seaborne raiders were already proving a
nuisance. Appreciable numbers of coin-hoards from the period 180–230 are
known in the eastern part of Britain, but not enough to add substance to the
assumption that the danger was exclusively from that region. During these
years, the majority of the towns of Britain were defended for the first time,
usually with a simple earthern rampart. Exceptions to this, surprisingly the
two large *civitas* capitals near the eastern coastline, are Canterbury and
Caistor-by-Norwich, both of which were still unwalled until the middle of
the third century. At Caistor, however, traces of earlier, probably earthwork,
defences on a different line from that followed by the stone walls suggest that
the site had not been totally undefended.

In addition, there is a growing body of evidence from sites in or near the
coastal regions of Essex and the south that some sites there were destroyed by
fire in the late Antonine period—at the very end of the second or the
beginning of the third century. At Chelmsford, a second-century defensive

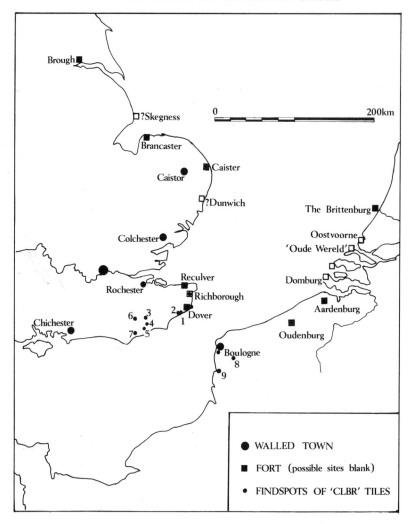

Fig. 10 Early third-century coastal sites in Britain and Gaul
(including findspots of *CLBR* tiles). The numbered sites are as
follows: 1, Folkestone; 2, Lympne; 3, Cranbrook; 4, Bodiam;
5, Beauport Park; 6, Bardown; 7, Pevensey; 8, Desvres; 9, Étaples.

ditch was deliberately filled in, partly with debris which included badly
burned, late second-century pottery. Similar finds of pits deliberately filled
with burnt debris of the same nature have been made at coastal and inland sites
between Colchester and London.[25] A total of more than ten sites have now
produced evidence of destruction at this period and it may be that here there is
evidence of a raid or a series of raids by barbarians or pirates some seventy
years before the historical sources record troubles in the coastal area.

Evidence for the continued existence of the *Classis Britannica* after the later second century is meagre: most of the specific finds seem to date from the second century. During the third, the fleet evidently ceased to function as effectively as before, for, by its end, Franks and Saxons were in control of the sea-lanes. There was probably some kind of defensive fleet operating in the Channel in the third century: a dedication from Arles records that an officer was Commander of the *Classis Britannica Philippiana*, which, since it bears the name of the emperor Philippus, must date the continued existence of the fleet to 245–7.[26] But the protection which such a fleet could afford was evidently becoming seriously limited.

One fixed point for our dating of the defences of the southern shores of Britain is the inscription found at Reculver recording the construction of one of the most important buildings within the fort—the shrine in the headquarters building and the cross-hall (*aedes principiorum cum basilica*)—in the early third century (Fig. 11).[27] The fort at Reculver has usually been regarded as earlier in style than its neighbours, and finds from the site and its surroundings have supported this assumption. The discovery of this inscription within the headquarters building of the fort itself was a find of major importance, for it dates the construction of the main building within the fort (and thus the completion of the fort itself) to the governorship of a man called Rufinus. There were two men in the early part of the third century

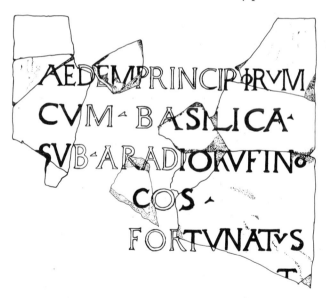

Fig. 11 The building inscription from the headquarters building
at Reculver. (After I. A. Richmond, *Ant. J.*, xl, 1960, 225.)
The translation runs: 'Fortunatus (built) the shrine in the
headquarters building with the cross-hall under the consular
governor? (Aradius) Rufinus'. Scale 1:4.

who may have been the governor here referred to: Aulus Triarius Rufinus, who could have been in Britain in the early years of the decade 210–20, and Quintus Aradius Rufinus, who could have been in Britain some fifteen years later, 225–30. Neither man is known to have had connections with Britain, and there were many Rufini in the third century who could have been Consul at Rome, followed by a term as governor of Britain. Rufinus was a common third- and fourth-century name, and the man named on the Reculver inscription need not have been either of the two Rufini we know of as consul from other sources.

Despite this, the plan and layout, such as it is known, at Reculver suggests that its design is earlier than the other coastal forts. The fort at Reculver is typologically almost exactly similar to that at Brancaster, where there is a similar picture of early finds from the fort's surroundings, though the fort itself has barely been touched by excavation. Although ploughing has reduced the remains at Brancaster to a bare minimum, such excavation as there has been inside the fort led to the conclusion that the earliest occupation there was not later than the middle of the third century. At Dover, too, the *Classis Britannica* fort was in use throughout the second century, and its life may have extended into the third.

The British system of coastal defences at this time comprised more than merely the forts of Reculver and Brancaster. The excavators at Caister-by-Yarmouth and Brough-on-Humber have both suggested that at these sites there was possibly a military or naval origin for the defences. Caister-by-Yarmouth in particular, with its rectangular plan and stone walls 3 m thick, replacing an earlier earth-and-timber defence, is typologically very similar to Reculver and of approximately the same size (Fig. 12). The stone walls, the construction of which is dated by the most recent excavations to the first half of the third century (but 'nearer 250 than 200 A.D.'), have a military character, which may be connected with the reorganization of the defences along the eastern coast.[28]

The same area provides other evidence. The stone defences at Colchester which predate the rampart bank found backing them (at least in one portion of the circuit) are probably of second-century date. The rampart-bank found in the excavations at St Mary's Rectory in Colchester is dated by the discovery beneath it of a house which was still in use in the period 170–200, whereas the wall at other parts of the circuit has been shown to date from the early second century.[29] Colchester was the showpiece colony for Roman civilization in Britain and so would naturally be among the first to receive new defences in stone. Though the provision of its walls in the first instance may have been in part an honorific gesture, the addition of a rampart bank behind the walls at about the turn of the third century may be a sign of more troubled times.

Bradwell, too, has produced finds which are earlier in date than the late

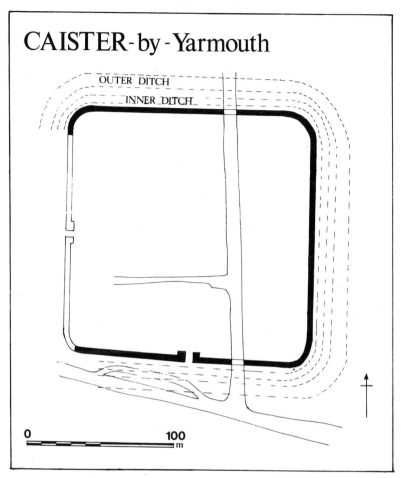

CAISTER-by-Yarmouth

OUTER DITCH

INNER DITCH

0   100
m

Fig. 12 Plan of the third-century stone walls of Caister-
by-Yarmouth. Scale 1:2500.

third century, the date at which the 'fort' walls were erected. The early finds belong to a phase of pre-fort settlement which was probably much more extensive than the later defended area. It is as well to recall that at Brancaster crop-marks of the second-century settlement are far more extensive than the fort site. Traces, albeit very slight, of similar rectangular (property?) boundaries have now been seen as crop-marks at Burgh Castle, some distance from the fort. There is a range of finds from Walton Castle, which suggests that it, too, was a township before the fort was placed there. Between Bradwell and Caister-by-Yarmouth on the coast lies Dunwich, commonly thought to be a likely site for the Roman town of *Sitomagus*, mentioned in contemporary itineraries. The Peutinger Table, a map of the Roman world, admittedly of fourth-century date, shows *Sitomagus* as a walled town. If it was a coastal site in the Roman period (coastal encroachment in medieval and modern times has virtually washed the site away) it may already in the late second century have formed part of a defensive chain.

Other sites elsewhere which may have belonged to this defensive scheme include the then newly defended port of Rochester, in Kent.[30] It is certain that towards the middle of the third century the monument at Richborough was converted into a lookout post defended by triple ditches and a clay rampart. At Lympne, reused material found in the later fort strongly suggests that there was here an earlier fleet-base later converted into a fortified harbour. The altar of Aufidius Pantera (Fig. 9, p. 15) was encrusted with barnacles, as if it had lain for some time under water before being hauled out and put to another use in the fort gateway.

Lost sites off the coast of Lincolnshire near Skegness may have linked the fort at Brancaster more closely with the coastline opposite the Wash.[31] This was one of the more important invasion routes into Britain, since it concealed the entrance to two easily navigable rivers, the Nene and the Witham, both of which were attractive routes inland for a seaborne enemy. Further north, on the Humber estuary itself, the site at Brough, long in use as an auxiliary fort, continued to be maintained as a fort-cum-base for the fleet; Brough was refortified with a new turf and timber rampart in about A.D. 200. It remained in military use certainly until 270, and may still have formed part of the coastal screen after that date.[32]

These fragments of evidence from sites along the eastern coasts of Britain in the earlier part of the third century are at present all that can be gleaned of the state of preparation for the crisis now threatening the island from the activities of pirates beyond the Rhine mouth. On the Continental side, there is some evidence that the warning of raids to come arrived somewhat earlier than in Britain: in 170, a tribe called the Chauci invaded *Gallia Belgica*.[33] As a result, towns which lay directly in the frontier areas began to build themselves walls—Trier and Tongres both have defensive circuits which date to this period[34]—though cities which lay a little further inland did not yet feel the need for such strong defensive action.

It is not until the middle of the third century that there is further evidence of renewed pressure on the coastal regions. Climatic change may well have been responsible for the desire of Franks, Frisians and Saxons to migrate southwards and attempt to fill the relatively vacant spaces inside the Roman empire: while Rome held a frontier and controlled territory inside it, she denied the use of vacant land to tribes who, in the middle years of the third century, were being harassed at home by loss of farming and settlement land because of the encroachment of the sea. In Friesland marine transgression was now beginning, forcing the abandonment of some of the settlements in the area as the inhabitants sought higher ground on which to live.[35] There is every indication, however, that despite the fact that it was low-lying, the area of land at the Rhine mouth was in no way threatened. It seems to have been stable, possibly even densely forested.[36]

The most important site on the Continent is probably represented by the earliest phase of the fort at Oudenburg. Near the middle of the third century, a fort was constructed and defended with an earthen rampart (see pp. 86–7). It lay near the sea-coast, some way south-west of the Rhine mouth and will have been in an ideal position to defend the coastal plain of Flanders. There is slight evidence for other forts extending in a chain along the coast of Holland as far as the Rhine mouth. At three sites, Domburg, Westerschouwen and Aardenburg, an unexpected rise in the numbers of coins in the period 260–73 attests exceptional activity, perhaps of a military nature, under Postumus.[37] Aardenburg itself was actually a fort. Its headquarters building and portions of the defensive circuit have been discovered.[38] Off the island of Goeree there lies a site called 'Oude Wereld', described by seventeenth-century antiquarian sources. On land which lies two kilometres to the south, excavations have un-covered what appears to be a military style *vicus* (a cluster of civilian buildings round a fort) which may be connected with this submerged site, for it has yielded tile-stamps which confirm a military connection.[39] On the north coast of the island of Walcheren, fragments of tile-stamps of the *Classis Germanica* suggest that here too, at the mouth of the Scheldt, there was an important base of strategic worth. Further sites, at Oostvoorne and the Brittenburg, which has not produced tile-stamps of the German fleet but a great deal of second- and third-century pottery, complete the picture. It is not certain how many of these sites were forts at this period: the evidence for most of them is extremely thin, but there is a good chance that some, if not all, were harbours used by a fleet which was attempting to form some sort of defence against the increasing pressure from the tribes who lived in the areas north of the Rhine mouth.

Further south, at Boulogne, clear indications of developments in the third century are lacking, but the port may have been walled at this time. Walls which run from the Haute Ville down to the water's edge may have been intended as a defence for the harbour, but as their discovery was recorded in the nineteenth century, the details of their dimensions, purpose, and relationship to the rest of the topography of Boulogne are vague.

There is no evidence for further forts on the coastline of Gaul south-west of Boulogne, but a series of important harbour sites on the main river estuaries may have formed the basis on which a Roman Channel fleet now operated. Of these, the most important lay at St Valéry sur Somme, Quend, Étaples, Wissant, and Calais-Marck. East of Calais, the coastline has changed considerably since Roman times and was probably changing during the Roman period itself. It is possible therefore that during some part of the

Roman period sites such as Ardres or Cassel may also have been near, if not actually on, the coast.[40]

The provision of new forts and the refurbishing of the existing defences of towns and settlements in the coastal areas of Gaul and Britain during the latter part of the second and the earlier part of the third centuries now begins to cohere into a rather more comprehensive picture than has before been recognized. It is difficult to ascertain the precise date at which the menace from barbarian sea-raiders first became really serious, but the cumulative effect of all this evidence cannot be ignored. The preparation of this series of defensive posts around the shores of the north-western corner of the empire strongly suggests that Roman military authorities were becoming aware that the threat from the Saxons was to grow stronger. But the lapse of control, the apparent ineffectiveness of the *Classis Britannica* during the third century, and the seriousness of the situation at the time when the Saxons were 'infesting the seas' formed a climax which even this series of prepared bases could not check. The failure of the Roman fleet to combat the problem of the Saxons in the third century was not represented by sudden defeat or by Roman abandonment of their attempts to maintain the peace and keep the trade-routes safe. The origins of the Roman failure are to be sought further back in the third century, in the inadequacy of the existing arrangements for the defence of the coastline and the constant, relentless pressure of the invaders.

By the third quarter of the third century, then, the existing bases were proving inadequate. The great invasion of 276 in Gaul brought repercussions also on the Channel coast, for there the threat of invasion was equally severe: the Saxons' mobility made them an enemy to be feared all along the exposed coastlines. This, then, is the setting into which we must place the construction of the new series of coastal forts, the extended system of defences which came to be known as the Forts of the Saxon Shore.

The recorded history of the Channel zone at this period is helped by the story of Carausius. We have already noted how in 259 Postumus headed a revolt against the legitimate emperor and his son, forming for a time the so-called 'Gallic empire'. A similar revolt, similarly headed by a military commander, Carausius, occurred in the coastal area in the latter part of the third century. This is, fortunately, well documented and is of importance in setting the historical framework of the period in which the new forts were built and the new strategy was conceived.

2 CARAUSIUS

The story of the Saxon Shore forts has long been associated with that of Carausius, so it is fitting to look first at the contemporary material telling of his usurpation, which created for a time in the late third century a separate empire in the island of Britain. Short, factual accounts of his reign are given by the late fourth-century authors Eutropius and Sextus Aurelius Victor, both most trustworthy and reliable sources. Bede and Orosius, in their histories of Britain, also mention the usurpation, but add nothing to the accounts of Eutropius or Victor; in fact their accounts appear to be taken, if not verbatim, at least in essence, from the earlier works.

Of other historical writers who covered the period, Nennius too contributes a paragraph, but this is somewhat wilder, and contains some errors which may be due to a misreading of Bede. The wildest account of all, by Geoffrey of Monmouth, which appears to be nothing more or less than complete fabrication, is much later and virtually worthless as a historical source for events of the late third century.

The other contemporary material for the story of Carausius comes from panegyrics, a collection of speeches in honour of the emperors of the Roman world at various times and places from the second to the fourth centuries. Four of these orations date to the latest years of the third century and were delivered before the emperor Maximian or his Caesar, Constantius. Of these, two in particular mention the revolt of Carausius: one given at Trier in 289, and the other at some unknown place, but probably Trier, in 297. The panegyrist's task is to praise the emperor, and Carausius is never mentioned by name, since he is always 'that pirate'—*ille pirata*—and receives treatment suitable for an enemy of the people. The campaigns of Maximian and Constantius to oust him from Britain are told in some detail, but how biased the account and how exaggerated the ease with which the British empire is supposed to have fallen are uncertain.

By 284, the dereliction of the Gallic provinces by successive claims to imperial power had exposed them not only to invasion from barbarians but also to a new threat. After the effacement of the effects of the big invasion of 276, the *Bagaudae* (see p. 3) had begun a type of brigandage which terrorized estates and towns throughout the province. Diocletian, now emperor, appointed Maximian, 'a trusted colleague although somewhat unrefined, and an experienced and gifted man', as general in charge of operations against the *Bagaudae*. At this point, Carausius first appears in the account as told by Victor:[1]

In this campaign, Carausius, a citizen of Menapia, made an outstanding contribution. For that reason, and because he was considered to have some knowledge of sailing (for in his youth he had been a steersman by profession), they put him in charge of preparing a fleet and clearing the sea of the Germans who were infesting it. In his overconfidence, since he was pressing many barbarians hard, but not transferring the captured spoils into the general treasury, in fear of Herculius [Maximian], by whom he learnt his death warrant had been issued, he seized Britain, and assumed imperial power.

Essentially the same story, with some extra details and some omissions, is told by Eutropius:[2]

At this period, Carausius, although a man of the lowest birth, had achieved great distinction through military service since he had accepted the commission at Boulogne to pacify the sea, which Franks and Saxons were infesting throughout the regions of *Belgica* and *Armorica*. Although he caught many barbarians, he did not give their spoils back intact either to the provincials or to the imperial treasury, and when he began to be suspected of allowing the barbarians in so that he could intercept them sailing past with their spoils and thus become rich, under sentence of death from Maximian he assumed the imperial power and seized Britain.

The suggestion that Carausius dealt improperly with the profits from his new-found naval power is thus embedded in the tradition which both Eutropius and Victor have taken over from some lost historian from whom they—and possibly also the *Historia Augusta*—took their information. It may represent the official version of a story which in reality was much less damaging to Carausius, at least in the eyes of the provincial Britons, than the one which we have. If Carausius was really letting the pirates land and collect booty, which he then recaptured while pocketing the proceeds, it is hard to see how his popularity among the moneyed classes could have been such as to strengthen his position as ruler of Britain in the following years.

Problems exist over the date of Carausius' usurpation, and also over the starting date of the command which he held. The sequence of Maximian's campaign against the *Bagaudae*, followed by Carausius' appointment as a result of his exploits in it, is clearly established by the historian. Maximian cannot have been appointed Caesar until after Diocletian became emperor in September 284,[3] and so the campaign against the *Bagaudae*, assuming it to be one of the first campaigns which the new regime had to undertake, began in late 284 or early 285. No direct evidence bears on the date when this campaign was undertaken, but a rather ambiguous reference in the panegyric of 291 has been thought to show that Maximian was already joint emperor with Diocletian when the campaign was begun.[4] Maximian's elevation came probably in March 286; but the passage says no more than that the Bagaudic rebellion forced the peoples of Gaul to apply for imperial help. It says nothing of the status of Maximian when he arrived to remedy the situation. The initial stages of the Bagaudic campaign, therefore, and the exploits of Carausius which earned him his promotion could have been over by mid 285, and this is the likely date for Carausius' assumption of the command of the Channel fleet.

The most likely date for the attempt by Carausius to become emperor is 286. Carausius was jealous of Maximian and considered that he had an equal right to the imperial position. By this time, with the Channel fleet well in his grasp, he considered himself at least the equal of Maximian. It may also be that the jealousy was not all one-sided. Maximian's death-sentence passed on Carausius for 'misuse of power' is perhaps an example of Maximian using his newly acquired position as a convenient means of getting rid of a dangerous and talented rival. That Maximian should attempt to eliminate Carausius by means of power which Carausius considered was rightly his, was insufferable. Carausius was forced into revolt.

The actual scope of Carausius' initial command is a matter of dispute (Fig. 13). Eutropius says that he accepted his command at Boulogne 'to pacify the

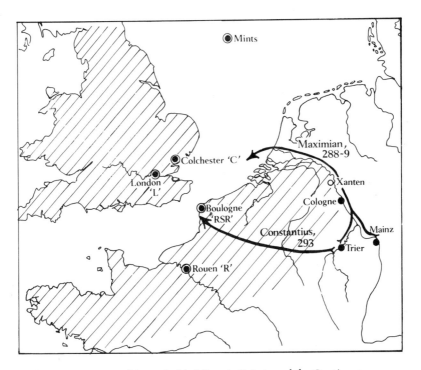

Fig. 13 Map of Carausius' holdings in Britain and the Continent, A.D. 286–93, showing the sites of his main mints and the two early campaigns by Maximian and Constantius to oust him.

sea throughout the regions of *Belgica* and *Armorica*'. It seems clear that for some part of his reign the empire of Carausius extended beyond the bounds of Britain. It is certain that up until 293, when the panegyrist joyfully records that Boulogne fell,[5] that port at least was in the hands of Carausius. There is also a mint-mark on some of the coins issued by Carausius which may mean that they were issued at Rouen; the Franks who lived at the Rhine mouth were also his allies. That he commanded wide areas of territory on the Continent is nowhere supported by the evidence, but if he had cleared the seas of the barbarians by 286, it is not unlikely that people who had previously lived in danger from them would have been in sympathy with him and yielded him support. His continued use of Boulogne and Rouen, and maybe other ports along the coast on which to base his fleet, is not surprising.

Nor is there any evidence that Britain was originally included in the command: the panegyrist of 297 says that Carausius took the fleet which once protected Gaul,[6] but this testimony is worth little, since he was trying to portray the crimes of Carausius in the worst possible light. Although there is no specific reference to Britain, it made little sense to defend the Gallic side of the Channel against raiders, while allowing them to attack the British side. The fleet must have served in some way to protect both sides: archaeological evidence for the destruction of villas and for the deposition of coin-hoards at this time shows that Britain and Gaul were equally threatened and equal prey to the barbarian raids.

It is also difficult to estimate how much support Carausius had. In 285, Diocletian assumed the title *Britannicus Maximus*,[7] which suggests that, during the period when Carausius' position was still legal in the eyes of the emperor, a victory of some description was won in Britain. It is just possible that Diocletian took over the title from Carinus, who had assumed it before him; yet it is unlikely that Diocletian, in his position of strength, should need to adopt this title merely as a propaganda measure. Either the British victory is a Carausian success against the sea-raiders, which, although perhaps not technically gained in Britain itself, would merit the description of a British victory, or it represents a success elsewhere in Britain, possibly against attacks from Pictish or Irish raiders. A series of coin-hoards and some destruction at Wroxeter dating to this period show that unrest and perhaps raiding were not confined to the eastern coastline. But by far the biggest and most important campaign in which Britain was concerned seems to have been the operation of Carausius against the barbarian raiders in the Channel. It is hard to imagine that the title assumed by Diocletian in 285 stemmed from some other, unrecorded, victory.

The troops of Britain, therefore, were likely to be well disposed towards Carausius as a good leader, if for no other reason; in addition, his enlistment of Gallic merchantmen in his navy, to which he added more ships (as we are told in the panegyrics),[8] presupposes no little support from the merchant classes. The pirate menace would have struck deep at their livelihood in the last few years. A competent commander with a fleet to reintroduce policing of the sea-lanes, which had been allowed to lapse since the days when the *Classis Britannica* flourished, would have seemed to promise the security they needed. The protection afforded to landowners and even town dwellers in the exposed coastal areas, parts at least of which were rich and prosperous, gave Carausius an added advantage.

The first task of a usurper is to win the support of as many of the population as possible. Donatives had to be issued to the troops and a method found of preserving the rich landowners' confidence, which had been won by successful control of the raiders. Both Eutropius and Victor stress that Carausius captured many of the barbarians and therefore he seems to have established effective control over their activities. But much the most important method by which Carausius attempted to gain influential support was by the issue of a strong coinage. Troops had to be paid; the coinage of the time was notoriously debased, with the result that the value of coin was decreasing. Carausius' new coinage, by increasing the metal content of the coins, possessed greater intrinsic value. This provided a secure basis for trade, as well as giving the troops, who were probably paid at least in part in Carausian coin, the confidence that their money would retain its full purchasing power.

The need for a stable currency had long been felt but attempts to introduce better coinage had apparently met with great opposition, since it involved the exchange of new coins for old at an unacceptable rate. As a unit, Britain

Fig. 14 *Left:* Head of Carausius from one of his coins. Scale 2 : 1.

Fig. 15 *Right:* Reverse type of Carausius coin, showing the legend *EXSPECTATE VENI*. Scale 2 : 1.

possibly had the mineral resources to stand an upgrading of the currency. This, together with the resources Carausius had from his capture of the raiders' spoils, helped to put his financial policy on a sound footing. Carausius' coins were at first an emergency issue: the death sentence passed on him would automatically mean that any army serving him would no longer receive pay from the state, and pay would be needed for them quickly. After a rather over-ambitious gold and silver issue, of which not many examples survive and probably not many were issued, the coinage stabilized with more solid precious-metal content, increasing its value and securing the economic position.

The combination of settled trading conditions and a new, more trustworthy coinage was the basis on which Carausius founded his popularity, and the coinage served a dual purpose in that it was also propagandist. One of his early issues, of which few examples survive, had a reverse with the legend *EXSPECTATE VENI*, 'come, we're ready' (Fig. 15), which is an allusion to a similar phrase in Virgil's *Aeneid*.[9] This literary misquotation would have lost much of the force of the imperative and the hopefulness of the inscription (which suggests, for those who read their Virgil,[10] some comparison between the exploits and aspirations of Carausius and those of Aeneas escaping from Troy and destined to found a new empire), unless it was circulated almost simultaneously or maybe even before the revolt: and it may be that the revolt was planned from some date earlier than early 286. Other coin legends are of a more traditional nature—*PAX BRITANNIAE*, 'peace in Britain', *RESTITUTOR BRITANNIAE*, 'the Restorer of Britain'—but perhaps were intended to have a subliminal effect on the British subjects and troops who received payment or used the coins for business transactions.

An important aspect of the coinage is presented by the legionary issues, which were possibly put out as donatives to the troops, and bore the names and titles of legions in the Roman army. As well as those for two of the British legions, the *II Augusta* and the *XX Valeria Victrix*, there exist coins for several Continental legions, including not only the *XXX Ulpia Victrix*, stationed at Xanten, and other Rhine legions, but also troops whose bases lay as far away as *Moesia*. These coins may be donatives for *vexillationes*—detachments of these legions serving with the North Gallic army at the time of Carausius' revolt. The panegyricist of 297 mentions a 'seized legion' held by Carausius. This may have been either the nearest legion to Britain, the *Legio XXX Ulpia Victrix*, or else a body of troops, not strictly a legion, formed of detachments of all the units which are commemorated on the Carausian coins. Other reasons for this coinage are not easily found, but it seems likely that Carausius had control of the *Legio XXX U.V.* His origins in the lowlands at the Rhine mouth suggest he may well have begun his military career in that legion; if so, its allegiance to him would only be natural.

At first, Maximian was kept occupied with raids across the Rhine itself and in attempting to pacify the tribes on the other side. Carausius had complete control of the Channel fleet and, as the Rhine fleet had suffered a disaster at the hands of German raiders some years earlier, there were no warships available for quick retaliation. The panegyrist in 289 says that because of good weather during the winter the new fleet being prepared on the Rhine and Moselle was in an advanced state of readiness, and that 'the pirate' had better watch out.[11] Obviously the objective of that year's campaigning season was a big assault to prise Carausius from his empire.

The silence maintained about the outcome in a speech delivered by the panegyrist of 291, possibly at Trier, is perhaps the most convincing evidence that the campaign of 289 did not go as planned.[12] In the later panegyrics, there is reference to bad weather being responsible for the failure of the expedition,[13] but it is quite likely that Carausius, with five years of sailing-experience in the Channel behind him, was more than a match for the newly raised, untrained fleet of Maximian. To his existing fleet Carausius added more ships, enlisting not only Gallic merchants but also Frankish mercenaries to man them.[14] Since Maximian's fleet had been built on the Rhine and Moselle, possibly at Trier and in the Koblenz region, his only line of approach to Britain was along the Rhine, passing peoples who were likely to be supporters of Carausius, and who, in the last three or four years, had needed fairly strict Roman control (Fig. 13, p. 25). It is even possible that Carausius, when this area was his, had settled Franks there deliberately to provide a buffer against Maximian's use of that route. It was Maximian's only way to the sea: with a large and well-trained fleet waiting at the mouth of the Rhine to give battle, Carausius must have felt in an invincible position.

This is reflected in the way in which, after the unsuccessful outcome of the

Fig. 16 Reverse type of Carausius coin, bearing the legend
CARAUSIUS ET FRATRES SUI. Scale 2 : 1.

expedition of 289, he now started to issue new coins, whose legends strongly suggest that he was aiming to establish his power on a more constitutional basis, through gaining the sanction of Diocletian and Maximian. Starting in 289 or 290, there is a series of coins which bear the busts of three emperors with legends such as *PAX AUGGG*—'Peace of the three Augusti'; there is even one issue which portrays the three busts with the inscription *CARAUSIUS ET FRATRES SUI*—'Carausius and his brother emperors' (Fig. 16). This is also possibly the time when Carausius adopted the names of Maximian, as a further honorific gesture, becoming 'Marcus Aurelius Mausaeus Carausius'. A further example of his attempts to secure recognition is seen in his adjustment of the coin-standard he was using to conform with that of the rest of the empire.

But all these attempts were to no avail. There was no official recognition by Diocletian, and the year 293, which saw the introduction of the Tetrarchy with its subdivision of the Roman empire into two separate parts, each ruled by an Augustus with a Caesar as deputy, ensured that there could be no recognition for the British usurper. In 293, Constantius was appointed Caesar in the western empire. He seems to have lost no time in attacking Carausius' Continental holdings.

The method chosen was no longer a direct assault on the island of Britain by sea, but an attack by land on the ports of the Gallic side of the Channel, and principally Boulogne. The campaign of Maximian which possibly ended in defeat at the Rhine mouth had exposed the dangers of attempting any similar direct assault. Once the emperor had selected the river or rivers on which to build his fleet, his attack would come from a predictable direction and could be met either at the mouth or by a blockade at some sympathetic port along the river. Since Carausius held some Continental territory, there can have been few rivers in Gaul from which it was safe to launch another seaborne attack. In any scheme of this nature, it was the element of surprise which was lacking; it is this which was uppermost in Constantius' plans for dealing with Carausius. The loyalist account is given by the panegyrist:

Immediately you arrived, Caesar, you were triumphant. Your speed of arrival, which anticipated all reports of your approach, trapped the supporters of that pirate faction, still persevering in their stupid allegiance, inside the walls of Boulogne, and deprived them of access to the sea which once had washed their gates. In this operation, your own providence and your ability which matched your planning were supreme; you rendered the whole inlet of the tidal harbour impassable by driving piles into the entrance passage and building a mole of stones in the way of shipping. So, by a stroke of genius, you gained complete tactical control, since the sea, advancing into the harbour, presented only a way of escape cut off; and by ceasing to return, as it were, it afforded no prospect of relief to the besieged.[15]

The stratagem worked: severed from the sea and all hope of rescue by Carausius, the garrison of Boulogne had to surrender. The whole of Gaul was now in Roman hands; an attack on Britain, once a fleet was built, could be launched from any port along the Channel coast and the island empire of Britain was more vulnerable than it had been for seven years. Constantius' campaign against the Franks at the Rhine mouth, which he undertook immediately after the recapture of Boulogne, added to the insecurity of Carausius' position. The latter paid dearly for the mistake of failure, for we are told that he was assassinated in 293 by his finance minister Allectus, who became ruler and emperor of Britain in his stead.[16]

It was now too late for a change of ruler to avert the end of the British empire. Attacks could be mounted, and strategy planned, over a much wider front than had before been possible, and whereas the British fleet under Carausius had formerly been capable of anticipating the direction of attacks from Maximian, now, under Allectus, this strategy no longer worked. It was impossible to patrol the whole coast of southern Britain; the Roman fleet might come from any direction and might be split into several parts. The only hope was to catch them at sea before arrival.

It took Constantius three years to build his fleet, and the extensive preparations which he made, including the establishment of a special mint at Meaux to finance the scheme, show that it was well planned. Time was on the Roman side; if the previous expedition of Maximian had ended in defeat, this was no doubt partly due to the unnecessary haste shown over the whole preparations. Constantius' attack was planned in two sections—Constantius, with his fleet, was to create a diversion in the Channel, while Asclepiodotus, with ships which appear to have been mainly troop-carriers, selected a landing point at a likely spot on the south coast. Possibly the expedition was fortunate in that it was not intercepted at sea, but what happened is told by the same panegyrist.

Our faith in your success, Constantius, was not disappointed. We have heard from stories told by your troops that, at just the right moment, a mist covered the surface of the sea so thickly that the enemy fleet, watching in ambush near the island of *Vectis*, was bypassed without them realizing it at all. They had no chance of stopping your attack, incapable as they were of resisting it.[17]

The Roman fleet reached land safely and, having done so, Asclepiodotus ordered his men to burn their boats and march for London. What happened on the other flank of the operation, with the diversionary fleet under Constantius himself, is uncertain, but Allectus fled, attempting to reach London and head off the attack on it.[18]

Fig. 17 Obverse of a gold solidus of Allectus, bearing the head of
the emperor. Scale 2 : 1.

Fig. 18 Ship types on reverses of coins of Allectus.
Scale 2 : 1.

Terrified, and seeing you at his heels, he panicked like a madman. Fatally failing even
to deploy his troops or arrange all the men he had brought with him for the battle, he
preferred to rush into the contest along with all the longstanding supporters of his
conspiracy and bands of German mercenaries, heedless of the preparations he had
made. It was a further gift made to the Roman empire, Caesar, that by your own
good fortune you won a victory for it with hardly the death of a single Roman. I
have heard it said that the plains and hills were covered with the corpses only of the
foulest of our enemies.[19]

In the midst of the field was found the body of Allectus, stripped of his
regalia and all sign that he had aspired to hold imperial rank. Constantius,
meanwhile, arrived at London with a relief force just in time to prevent its
capture and sack by the now leaderless bands of German mercenaries, who
were doubtless prepared to make the most of their situation while the going

was good. A medallion, struck to commemorate the recapture of Britain, describes Constantius as *REDDITOR LUCIS AETERNAE*—'the Restorer of eternal light', and it shows a picture of the personification of London kneeling to receive Constantius riding in on horseback (Fig. 19). After ten years the usurpation was over.

Fig. 19 The Arras medallion: the people of London welcome the returning Caesar Constantius.

3 THE BRITISH FORTS

Of the series of forts which rings the southern and eastern coasts of Britain, only a few have been closely examined. Probably the most famous excavations were those carried out at Richborough, the publication of which still forms a valuable corpus of material of all periods from a Romano-British site. Here, almost the whole of the interior of the fort and its ditches has been excavated and laid out to view: most of the features now visible, however, date from periods earlier than the construction of the strong 'Shore fort' walls.

Less comprehensive excavation has taken place at other forts. In recent years, research excavation at Portchester has been directed at examining a portion of the walled area, and at Dover, rescue work in advance of the new town by-pass located not only the late Roman fort, but also an earlier Roman naval base. Reculver has been the subject of a continuing series of excavations for a number of years. Earlier examination of Burgh Castle and Pevensey was in no way comprehensive, and at the other accessible forts there have only been small, trial excavations.

Brief accounts now follow of the state of knowledge of all the British forts, in order from Brancaster on the Wash to Portchester near Southampton Water.

Brancaster

This fort is situated on the north Norfolk coast, at present about a mile from the sea but originally presumably on an estuary which was navigable. It was also not very far from the line of two Roman roads—the Peddar's Way, running north-south, and another road running east-west across the top of East Anglia. In the seventeenth century, the walls were mentioned as still standing twelve feet high, surrounded by an eighteen-foot ditch, but the fort was demolished systematically in 1770, leaving only the foundations for study today. The walls are 2·70 m thick and enclose an area roughly 170 m square with rounded corners. The wall is backed by a rampart, 6 metres wide. A berm of 12 m separates the wall from the ditch, 13·5 m wide and 2·40 deep. Early excavations at the north-east corner had found the wall 3·30 m thick, faced with sandstone, and with an angle tower containing a small room, 2·70 by 2·10 m. All the walls rest on a foundation-course of loose flints and sand, while the main wall has at least one bonding course of sandstone, apparently below ground-level.

The north-west corner, examined in 1933, had an internal rectangular tower, which must have meant a break in the rampart bank. Traces of wooden shuttering for the walls were also found. The core of the wall was of flint, ironstone and hard chalk rubble set in concrete, built with the technique of pouring separate layers of hard-setting mortar over rubble debris laid between the inner and outer faces of the wall. The rampart of sand, presumably dug to create the fort ditch, contained no residual material, though there were traces of a charcoal layer underlying it in some places. Inside it, a strip of chalk pitching 3·50 m wide was found, presumably the *intervallum* road, in which, wedged between the stones, was a coin of 270. At one point, a rubbish dump overlay the rampart bank and part of the chalk-pitched road: the deposit of this rubbish was dated after 273 by the discovery of a coin buried in it.

The west gate of the fort was in extremely poor condition. The gap for the gate was 12 m wide and only a slight inward turn of a wall was found to show the emplacement of a guard chamber. The rest had been thoroughly robbed out. Relying on a spread of rubbish both inwards and outwards from the gate

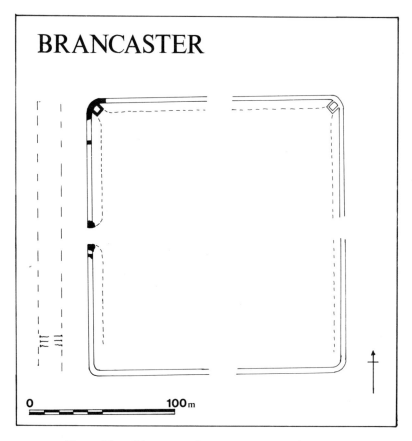

Fig. 20 Plan of the Roman fort at Brancaster. Scale 1:2500.

Fig. 21 Aerial view of the fort at Brancaster, showing the lines of
streets of the civilian settlement beyond the fort site.

at this point, J. K. St Joseph, the excavator, suggested that there may have
been external gate-towers. It is true that the excavator in the mid nineteenth
century reported that at the east gateway the 'bastions' had been obliterated,
but there is no evidence to show that he meant projecting towers rather than
internal guardrooms.

Relatively recent discoveries have shown (Fig. 21) that the fort site is but a
small part of the extensive settlement area. Crop-marks show that there was
an extensive settlement, formed of enclosures and roads, both east and west of
the fort site, and apparently aligned, not on the fort itself, but on a smaller
double ditched enclosure nearer the water's edge. Excavation has shown that
the dating of these enclosures is predominantly of late second- and early
third-century date. The fort itself, therefore, appears to have been built over
an earlier existing settlement, and to have superseded it completely.
Excavation has not located traces of later third- and fourth-century
settlement.

Despite being a fort which appears typologically early, therefore, and having internal corner (and gate?) towers, a rampart backing to the walls and the *intervallum* road, Brancaster can scarcely date much earlier than the second quarter of the third century. The majority of the coins found in excavation in the 1930s came from between A.D. 250–300, thus leading the excavator, St Joseph, to claim that the first significant occupation of the fort dated from the later years of the fourth century. Occupation continued at least until the reign of Theodosius, since six of his coins have also been found. The interior of the fort, which should give some indication of the periods of occupation on the site, has not yet been systematically examined.

Burgh Castle

Burgh Castle stands on a tributary of the Yare River, the River Waveney, at the summit of ground steeply sloping down to estuary—or river—level. Three sides of the fort-walls are still standing, while the western one, along the top of the slope, has fallen, and no trace can today be seen. In Roman times, the estuary was much wider than Breydon Water is now and may well have extended from the site of present-day Yarmouth as far inland as Caistor-by-Norwich. From the site, situated some four miles inland, there is no direct view of the sea and in Roman times it would have been difficult of land-access too, since it was situated in the 'Lothingland', which, apart from being dense forest, was also virtually cut off from the mainland by tracts of inland water.

The east wall of the fort is 200 m long and runs roughly parallel to the line of the escarpment on the western side. The north and south walls are each about 90 m long and give the fort a trapezoidal shape, with rounded corners and external towers. The walls are about 3·50 m thick at foundation level, but appear, though much robbed, to be stepped back on the inside face, decreasing to only 1·30 m thick at the top, which is 4·30 m above ground level. Tile-courses on the interior face of the walls at irregular intervals show that the facing was stepped back in this way. The walls are built of a facing of split flints, interrupted at five-course intervals by triple rows of tiles, round a concrete core, which is of hard white mortar though the facing stones are pointed with a mortar tinged pink by the admixture of crushed tile. The foundations rest on a timber framework, the beam-holes of which have been recognized at various points around the circuit.

Excavations were carried out in 1850 and 1855 to try to trace the west wall: at the bottom of the hill were found the traces of foundations, but judging from more recent work which has located the missing wall at the top of the slope, these must have been harbour works. The same nineteenth-century excavations located the site of the main east gate into the fort and showed that it was a single portal, 3·50 m wide, with a timber threshold, but no trace of any outworks at all. Running back inside the fort from the gateway were

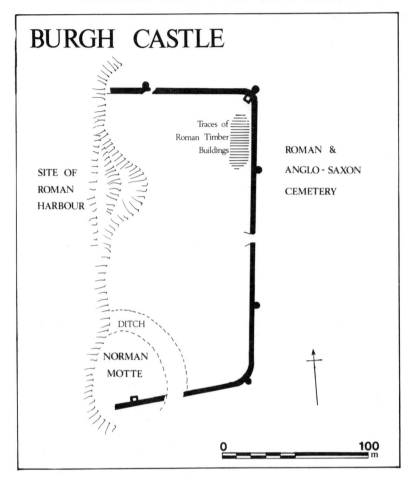

BURGH CASTLE

Traces of
Roman Timber
Buildings

ROMAN &

ANGLO - SAXON

CEMETERY

SITE OF

ROMAN

HARBOUR

DITCH

NORMAN

MOTTE

0   100
                                             m

Fig. 22 Plan of the Roman fort at Burgh Castle. Scale 1 : 2500.

found two 'retaining' walls, designed, as the excavator thought, to prevent the earth in the rampart from spilling out into the gateway. There is also a postern gate in the north wall, protected by a flanking bastion.

Recent research has located a corner turret at the north-east angle which was contemporary with the building of the fort, but which had been demolished later: traces of lean-to buildings were also found against the interior of the walls. If the walls had an earth bank behind them, therefore, as part of the fort's original plan, it must have been removed fairly early on. An earth bank, 3·50 m wide, behind these thick walls would not be unparalleled among the Saxon Shore forts, but it is more likely that the 'revetment' walls at the east gate were the walls of guard chambers, and if so the evidence that an earth rampart ever existed disappears.

Round the exterior of the walls are projecting horseshoe towers, about 4 m in diameter. For the first 2·20 m of their height above ground level they are not bonded into the wall of the fort, though the tile-courses are of exactly the same height and type as those in the walls (Fig. 23). At and above this height of 2·20 m there appears to be a curved mortar surface sloping down over the core of the wall to the outside facing, over which the bastion facing continues back into the interior of the wall. Above this height, the towers are more securely bonded in; but the tower and wall tile-courses were still not always properly interleaved as is shown by the tower on the north wall, where the tile-courses do not coincide. The towers, set at the fort corners, midway along the short sides, and between the corners and the east gate on the east wall, all have a hole 0·60 m in diameter in the top of them, often presumed to be for some kind of *ballista*. Survey of the corner bastions has shown that in their present form they could hardly have provided cross-fire along the fort walls, since because of the curve of the wall at the corner they do not project beyond the line of either of the walls, and therefore cannot have enfiladed them.

No breaks indicating building sections are immediately visible: the walls

Fig. 23 Exterior tower of the fort at Burgh Castle: note the straight bond between tower and fort wall (*left*).

are extremely riddled with cracks, presumably caused by the ivy which protected the topmost courses for so long from being robbed. But it is unlikely that the cracks are caused by structural defects—for example, breaks at the junction of building sections. The layering of slightly different colours of mortar in the wall-core is visible at various places where the facing has been robbed away and these mortar layers continue uninterrupted across many of the cracks in the wall facing. The tiles are small, some 200 by 30–40 mm; but larger ones, up to 320 mm long, are also found. Tile-courses are spaced evenly and, though variations in the number of flint courses between them do occur in the different parts of the wall, the facing is so robbed that it is impossible to tell where the joins between them come.

Excavations in 1958–61 by Charles Green examined two main areas within the fort walls. At the north-east corner, a series of trenches revealed insubstantial traces of mortar floors, possibly belonging to timber-framed Roman buildings with wattle-and-daub walls. These had burnt down, and were covered by layers of clay and debris which could have formed a platform for further timber buildings, all trace of which had been lost in the ploughsoil. One of these buildings lay right against the interior of the fort wall, and a series of indentations cut through the lowest courses of the wall in this corner are its only surviving trace. Pits and post-holes in the area gave some indication of later Middle Saxon (seventh or eighth century) occupation, though the nature of this was not entirely clear. The dating evidence recovered from the Roman buildings puts their destruction firmly in the middle years of the fourth century. A remarkable series of coin hoards, all of remarkably similar date around the decade A.D. 330–340 was found buried among these debris layers, which were also rich in pottery finds.

The other main area examined was the south-west corner, the site of a Norman motte, levelled in the mid nineteenth century. Here a Roman masonry building was found lying next to the fort wall, and traces of an interval turret were also discovered. Above the rubble of this building, there were fragmentary traces of later floors, but the topmost portion of these deposits had been very much disturbed by the levelling of the Norman earthworks. To the north of this building lay an extensive cemetery, containing adults and children, very shallow under the present surface, and producing nothing with the bodies to ascertain its date. There is a tradition that the site of Burgh Castle was the place 'Cnobheresburg' given by King Siehgbert of the East Angles to the Irish St Fursey for the foundation of his monastery in A.D. 630. This cemetery, and the traces of a wooden building nearby, were eagerly identified by the excavator as the monastic cemetery and church of St Fursey. It is by no means certain, however, that this building or the graves are of middle Saxon date: they are certainly pre-Norman, but the discovery that abandoned Roman forts might have late Roman churches in them may cast some doubt on the middle Saxon identification.

The field to the east of the fort is the known site of an early Saxon and probably Roman cemetery. No excavation has been done here, though ploughing has turned up Saxon burial urns; the site may one day provide an important and coherent link between the late Roman and the early Saxon occupations of the fort.

Walton Castle

On the borders of Essex and Suffolk, near the mouths of three rivers, the Stour, Orwell and Deben, which today reach the sea near the port of Harwich, there once stood another fort of the Saxon Shore type at Walton, near Felixstowe. Documentary evidence shows that a walled site fell down the cliff in the eighteenth century and that it once stood 100 feet above sea level.

The evidence for the existence of the site at Walton Castle is a series of sketches of the fort. One of the most distinctive, made from a print of an earlier drawing, shows the ruins of a circular bastion on the edge of the cliff, evidently that of the one at the south-west corner of the station, with a small portion of the south wall running seawards and overhanging the precipice. A tracing (Fig. 24) also exists from a pen and ink outline drawing of 1623, showing a view of the east wall of the fort, which at first sight might easily be mistaken for Burgh Castle. It shows a length of wall, with a gap in the middle

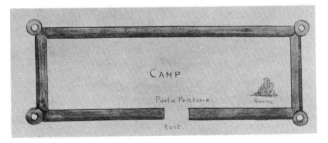

Fig. 24 Plan and drawing (from a seventeenth-century source) of the lost fort at Walton Castle.

for the gateway, and with a round bastion at each end. Cracks are visible in the walls, as at Burgh, and the lower portions of the corner towers are very much robbed away, in this respect also presenting an appearance very similar to those at Burgh. Underneath the drawing is a rough sketch-plan of the fort—a rectangle, approximately three or four times as long as it is wide, with a round tower at each corner—a most unusual shape for a Roman fort, even on the Saxon Shore. The drawing seems to show the cliff-line in the foreground, which would mean that the whole of the fort was then on top of the cliff. But the drawing from which the tracing was made is of doubtful authenticity, even though the signature, which is also copied, is orthographically correct for the sixteenth century.

Literary references to the fort are found in the Minute Books of the Society of Antiquaries of London. The description of 1732 runs 'tis 100 yards long, 5 feet above ground, 12 feet broad at each end and turned with an angle. It is composed of pepple and Roman bricks in three courses, all round footsteps of the buildings, and several large pieces of wall cast down upon the strand by the seas undermining the cliff, all which have Roman brick'. Later, in 1735, the fort is described as 187 yards long, with walls nine feet thick. Such a discrepancy in the basic size of the fort leaves much to be explained; but, if the description is to be relied on, the facing and the stonework were very similar to those of other forts of the Saxon Shore.

Enough finds have been made in the vicinity of Walton Castle to show that there was an extensive settlement during much of the Roman period; coin-finds seem to indicate a long period of occupation. The site was probably in long use as a *vicus*, if not as a port, and the fort emplacement seems typical of the late third-century strengthening and fortification of such ports as did exist. The harbour of Harwich has changed much in outline since the seventeenth century, and it is possible that much more of it was shingle in Roman times. The position where the fort stood is now open sea, but it may well once have commanded a good harbour at the river-mouths.

In a synopsis of Roman sites in Suffolk, I. E. Moore doubts whether the remains at Walton were a Saxon Shore fort in view of the discrepancy between the two eighteenth-century descriptions of their size and the lack of pictorial evidence in original form. But whereas it may be impossible to trust the detail of accounts of the remains, the evidence seems to be clear that a fort of Saxon Shore type stood here. Moore compromises by saying, 'It seems better to regard Felixstowe as the site of an extensive commercial settlement and port, though the possibility of its having received a small garrison, or indeed, having been the base for a naval detachment cannot be ruled out'. How this description differs from that of a known Saxon Shore site, like Richborough, in the late third century, it is difficult to see: Richborough, too, had an extensive settlement outside the walls, and was presumably equally important as a commercial port and as a base for the fleet and the army. But it was not just mere trading-posts which were provided with this type of defence: the most notable ports were defended both to harbour the fleet and to protect shipping. The construction of a defensive circuit at this time at Walton Castle can only mean that it was intended as one of the Saxon Shore forts.

Bradwell

The site lies very near the edge of marshy ground next to the sea at the north-east corner of the promontory south of the River Blackwater in Essex. Only three sides of the fort now remain, the fourth (seaward) side having been undermined by the waves. The south wall is the best preserved; on the site of the main west gate stands the Saxon Chapel of St Peter, dated to 652 and built predominantly of Roman material. Like Burgh Castle, the north and south walls of the fort are not parallel, and so the fort was not rectangular. The surviving walls enclose five acres (2 hectares).

Various excavations (see Fig. 26) have been carried out on the site since 1864, when the remains were first discovered and examined. Because of the very acidic nature of the soil, little has survived, and the walls have been almost completely flattened, probably by cultivation. The fragment of wall still visible on the south side is faced with tiles in triple courses and with septaria nodules—about the only local kind of building material. In 1865, the wall was reported to be 'upwards of 14 feet thick, and on the west side are foundations of two towers, one semicircular, one of horseshoe form'. Similar towers are presumed to have existed all round the circuit, but have not been located. The foundations of the wall are composed of boulders and rough stones and the core is of rubble concrete. The north-west angle bastion is 4·5 m in diameter, projecting 3·90 m from the wall. The interval tower is 38 m south of the north-west corner.

A section cut more recently across the defences 20 m north of the chapel showed that there was an offset course of tiles on the exterior of the fort wall at ground level, as at Burgh (see Fig. 23 and Fig. 57, p. 99). Both faces of the wall had a recess below ground level, as if the whole wall had been laid in wooden shuttering. No trace of any interior rampart was found, but 'a roll in the ground behind the north and west walls, and a mass of yellow clay behind the south wall indicate its existence'. The ditch was sectioned, but no precise outline of its shape was recoverable. A notable find from the bottom of the ditch was pottery of the pagan Saxon period.

Some interior buildings were found in the nineteenth century, near the south wall, but no pattern or sense was made of them. There also exist some fragments of what may be a Roman harbour connected with the site some

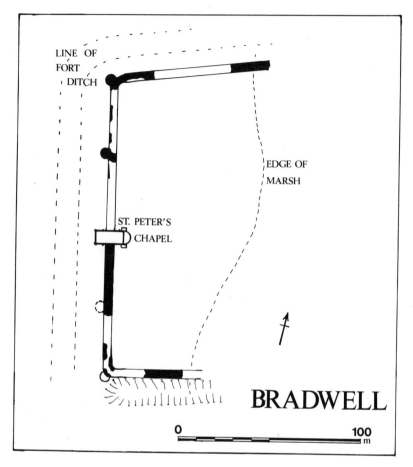

Fig. 25 Plan of the fort at Bradwell. Scale 1 : 2000.

distance out in the marshland, visible, according to local reports, as submerged masonry outlines.

The coin-series from Bradwell is similar to that of Pevensey; when drawn in histogram form, it shows that most coins found fall in the period 306–64, the majority being Constantinian. But, as usual, we are dealing with minimal numbers of coins: the main issues found are those of Carausius (286–93), Constantine (305–21) and Theodosius, and there is a fairly full series from Saloninus (259) onwards. The histogram does not necessarily tie Bradwell down to a date comparable with that of Pevensey whose coin pattern it most closely resembles. The shortage of evidence naturally makes such a coin-series unrepresentative.

Fig. 26 Line-drawing of the nineteenth-century excavations at Bradwell.
The view is from the interior of the fort, looking towards the east
end of St Peter's chapel. Note its ruined apse just visible as a
foundation.

Reculver

Just under half of the fort at Reculver has been washed away by the sea, but in Roman times it was nearly square, with rounded corners, about 180 by 175 m. The walls are 3 m thick and have an earth bank behind them: no bastions are known, nor are there any tile-courses in the walls. Only the core of the walls survives, since the facing stones have been robbed away, but at one point a large jutting repair has filled a gap in the walls. Only two gateways still survive: both southern and eastern gates have only a single turret. No details are yet recorded of any internal corner towers, but excavation has found some of the interior buildings, notably the *principia*, and two other 'living quarter' buildings next to it. Sections across the defences have shown that the fort had two ditches, which had begun to silt up quite early in the fort's life.

Underneath all the buildings and occupation layers of the early third century have been found the remains of a Claudian ditch. This suggests that the fort was on the emplacement of a garrison of the earliest occupation phase of the island, and that here was a fort or fortlet belonging to the actual invasion period. Evidence for Claudian military occupation in Kent is sparse and is virtually unknown apart from the double ditches on the Richborough peninsula. Reculver provides a much needed twin to Richborough, making the Wantsum channel a well-guarded harbour for the fleet which, until the

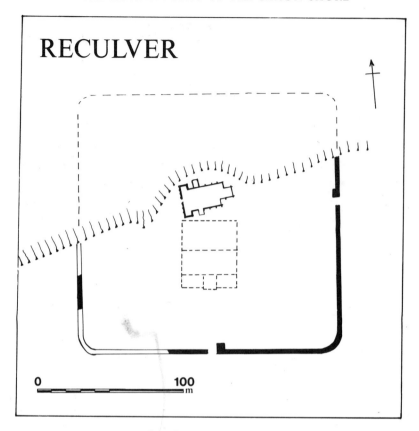

Fig. 27 Plan of Reculver fort. Scale 1:2500.

soldiers could become established, was a very important factor in bringing supplies as well as reinforcements.

There is little published evidence for the occupation phase of the fort at Reculver. A series of pits and well-bottoms found to the west of the fort, all of the late second or early third century, show that the settlement was more extensive in Roman times than merely the area of the fort. The land is said to have extended more than half a mile seaward in the Roman period, and the Roman town of Reculver is now swallowed up by the sea. It is worth noting that the orientation of the *principia* presupposes the main fort-entrance to be from the north (the *via praetoria*). There may thus have been a settlement and probably a port at Reculver before the Saxon Shore fort was put there. Because of coastline movement, it is impossible to tell whether there was a harbour to the north of the fort: the River Wantsum, curving behind Reculver in a long inlet, would seem to have been a more suitable place to

Fig. 28 Reculver towers: the remains of St Egbert's twelfth-century
church within the Roman fort.

choose, but no excavation to test this has taken place. Built probably about
225, two of the buildings near the *principia* appear to have been in ruins by the
beginning of the fourth century, but there is apparently no mention of
reoccupation of any part of the site. However, late third-century material is
common and the mention of the fort and its garrison in the *Notitia* show that
occupation continued into the later years of the fourth century, as coin-finds
confirm. After a period of Carausian occupation, the fort appears to have lain
for some time in disuse and quantities of rubbish collected inside it. The
reoccupation of the fort at some date in the fourth century was of a far more
temporary nature. Roads and buildings of the third-century fort appear to
have been buried by rubbish and the strong room of the *principia* had been

filled with building debris to level it off, preparatory to reuse; most of the buildings, however, seem to have been timber structures. The coin-series stops at about 360, which is very early by comparison with that of Richborough, where by far the greatest proportion of coins found date after this period.

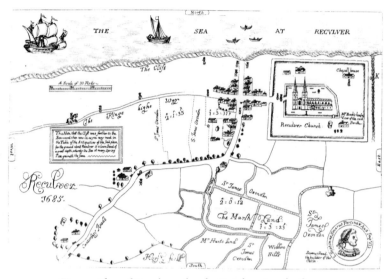

Fig. 29 Plan of Reculver, dated 1685, showing the fort as a rectangular enclosure containing the church and various associated buildings.

Richborough

The site is set on a knoll which was a peninsula in Roman times. The fort walls, which belong to one of the later phases of occupation on the site, describe a rectangle, the eastern side of which has now collapsed into the River Stour. But parts of the walls preserve a height of some 8 m, particularly those on the west.

After being a Claudian supply base and, later in the same century, the site of a triumphal arch recording the conquest of Britain, the port of Richborough seems to have been eclipsed, in the early third century, by its nearest rival, Dover. The character of its occupation appears to have been exclusively civilian at this time, but it is likely that towards the middle of the century the monument was converted into a look-out post; triple ditches (two of which, however, avoid a house already standing to the north-east) were dug to enclose a small area of about one acre round it. The next phase of building on the site is represented by the stone walls of the Saxon Shore fort, for the construction of which the whole site had to be levelled.

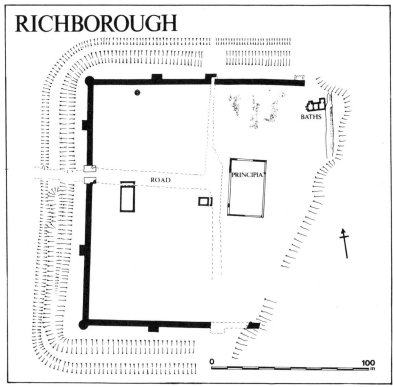

RICHBOROUGH

BATHS

ROAD

PRINCIPIA

0 100 m

Fig. 30 Plan of the fourth-century remains at Richborough.
Scale 1: 2330.

These walls are 3·30 m thick, built of small ashlar and double tile-courses enclosing a concrete core. External towers, set midway between gates and corners of each wall, are rectangular; at the corners there are three-quarters round towers. The north gate is a postern which defends a right-angled passage through the wall, while the west gate is a single portal flanked by two rectangular towers built of reused large stones from the monument. Reused material of all sorts is known from the walls. The fort was surrounded by double ditches, except at one point on the west, where a third ditch was dug out of alignment with the others 'by mistake'.

Levelling of the site for the construction of the walls meant the filling of the triple ditches and the demolition of what was left of the monument: broken marble fragments in the walls and the ditch-fillings show that it was already in disrepair. Fortunately, the filling of the triple ditches of the early fort, levelled for the construction of the stone-built fort, is datable by archaeological evidence. The foundation for a projected east wall of the fort which was later abandoned (the east wall as built being placed some distance further east) sealed the fill of the inner ditch but at the same time cut through the remains of

Fig. 31 The north wall of the fort at Richborough. Note the patterning used by one of the building gangs (*right*) and the plain masonry used by another (*left*).

the second-century house; here the outer two ditches had previously stopped short. This unused wall-footing was later itself cut by a pit. This happened long enough after it had been laid down for three feet of debris to have accumulated above the foundation and evidently long enough after its construction for its presence to have been forgotten. In the fill of the pit were 130 coins: twenty-two of these belong to the period 254–73 and none is definitely assignable to a later date. This evidence suggests that the wall foundation was constructed and the ditches of the earlier fort filled in prior to the usurpation of Carausius (286–93). The absence of Caurausian coins from the filling of the ditches (apart from one coin, found in dubious circumstances) as well as from this obviously later pit would be very surprising if the fort was built in his reign.

The existence of this abortive east wall-foundation is an interesting element in an examination of the sequence of construction phases at Richborough. There are a number of discrepancies and peculiarities about the walls of the fort (see Fig. 30): the south and west walls are not in rectangular alignment with the north wall and the north part of the west wall; irregular putlog holes, which do not coincide with similar holes lower down the wall, show different phases of construction where scaffold posts had to be replaced; the ditch 'dug in error' on the west side was a costly and uncharacteristic mistake for a military builder; the bastion at the south-west corner, to judge from the irregular tile-course round it and from the engraving which clearly shows the fort wall continuing straight behind the bastion (Fig. 58, p. 101), was added on after the fort walls were built. In addition, the alignments of several features of the site fail to correspond in a number of ways, which suggests that the process of building was long-drawn-out.

The time taken over the building programme is difficult to assess, but it was probably several years' work. The evidence of a pit (or well) shaft cutting the unused east wall foundation seems to suggest that there were substantial time-lags between the building of the various phases.

Excavation produced little evidence of any structures associated with the Saxon Shore fort: there was a small bath-house in the north-east corner, on the site of the second-century house already mentioned; two buildings, similar in plan but of uncertain purpose, perhaps temples or guild-halls, lie elsewhere in the fort and are contemporary with it. In the centre, the massive platform of the monument was levelled, and its foundation used as a base for a rectangular building which may have been the fort's headquarters. Other-wise, the interior buildings were wooden barrack blocks, which left little trace; their existence can only be deduced with difficulty from reports of the fort's original excavation in 1926–31.

Later still, probably in the early fifth century, a Christian church was constructed of timber and daub in the north-west corner of the fort. An enigmatic structure, till recently unrecognized, is now known to have been a baptismal font (see p. 152). Most significant, however, in this later period is the massive increase in coin-finds belonging to the reigns of Theodosius and his sons (402–10) which is in total contrast to what is found at other Saxon Shore forts; these coins show that Richborough continued to be the centre of important activity well into the fifth century.

Dover

Nothing was known of the site of the Saxon Shore fort of Dover until 1970, when rescue excavations in advance of a new trunk road located not only a corner of the Saxon Shore fort, but also extensive remains of an earlier fort, dating from the earlier second century.

It is now clear that the Saxon Shore fort of Dover lay on the west bank of the Dour estuary, on ground overshadowed by high hills to the south-west. The south and west walls of the fort have been located, and join at an obtuse angle. The south wall, 2·42 m thick, built of tufa and chalk blocks, extends at least 120 m eastwards from its junction with the west wall. This also was traced a similar distance, running parallel to the former estuary which follows roughly the line of the main road through the centre of Dover. Within about 5 m of this wall was the fort-ditch. Several external towers have been found: the one at the corner of the west and south walls is fragmentary and very much disturbed by later buildings and pits. At a distance of 30 m along the west wall were the chalk and flint foundations of a semicircular tower sitting on the lip of the ditch and added to the wall. Further towers were found on the south wall, spaced at about 25 m intervals from the south-west corner. The construction of at least one of these towers was quite different from that of the wall: a double tile-course ran round it, and the chalk blocks of its facing were much cruder than the actual fort wall. It stood on a chamfered plinth, though the wall did not, and clearly it, too, was secondary to the fort's construction.

Behind the wall of the fort was piled a bank of earth to give access to the walls and to provide extra strengthening to the defences. The presence of this bank had buried and thus preserved several rooms of an earlier house with painted wall-plaster, while the foundation trench for the wall had been dug right through the floor of one of its rooms. The existence of this bank, and the fact that the Shore fort, as first built, had no towers (though no trace of an internal angle turret was found either) suggest obvious parallels with such a site as Burgh Castle. A preliminary report suggests the fort was built in the second half of the third century.

As well as destroying, and thus ironically preserving, part of the house with painted wall-plaster, the fort and its ditches cut across the emplacement of an earlier fort of more regular Roman plan. Evidence of tile-stamps shows that this fort belonged to the *Classis Britannica* and was probably its British headquarters. Much of the plan has been found: the fort was rectangular with rounded corners, and contained many barrack blocks built of chalk masonry, separated by gravel roads. The north gate lay on the line of the later ditch of the Saxon Shore fort, which had destroyed the eastern gate-tower. This early fort was situated to the south and west of the later one, and must have been in ruins at the time of its construction, since the wall of the late third-century fort cuts through the barrack blocks of the earlier one. The *Classis Britannica* fort walls were 1·17 m thick, and apparently were not backed by a rampart, since the barrack-type buildings (some of them containing fragments of wall-plaster) seemed to butt up almost to the wall itself. Here and there, the latter showed unusual decorative patterning in chalk and tufa blocks; it was bounded by a large shallow V-shaped ditch. Harbour installations at Dover are already known from other excavations, and it therefore appears that during the second century at least, and again at the end of the third century, Dover was an important port for military traffic. Outside, spacious houses

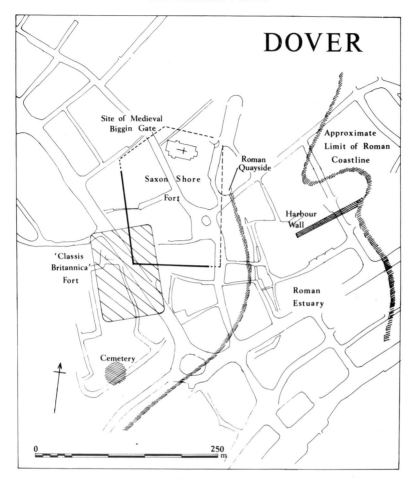

DOVER

Site of Medieval
Biggin Gate

Approximate
Limit of Roman
Coastline

Roman
Quayside

Saxon Shore
Fort

Harbour
Wall

'Classis
Britannica'
Fort

Roman
Estuary

Cemetery

0   250
                                       m

Fig. 32 General plan of Dover, showing the *CLBR* fort, the
Saxon Shore fort and the estuary of the River Dour
as it may have been in Roman times. Scale 1:5000.

provided living quarters for officers or tradesmen. When pirates threatened, the new Saxon Shore fort was built much nearer to the harbour, and, as a measure of the urgency of the situation, was cut through the rather more opulent civilian houses as well as the disused military installations.

Lympne

Set in tumbled masses on the slope of a steep hill which drops down to the marshlands at sea level, Stutfall Castle at Lympne is in some ways the most unusual of the forts. Its walls trace an irregular pentagon with the southward side now bounded by the Royal Military Canal, which runs along the edge of

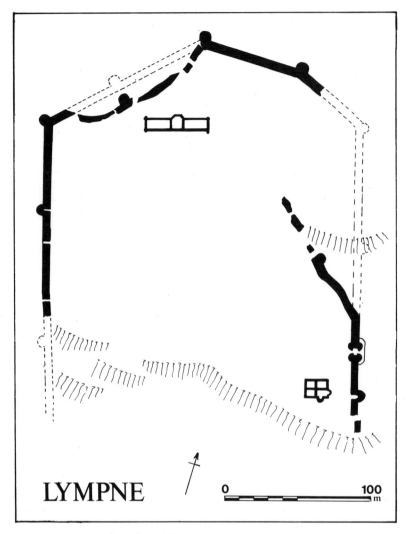

Fig. 33 Plan of Stutfall Castle, the Roman fort at Lympne.
Scale 1 : 2500.

Romney Marsh; this was perhaps the limit of the sea-shore in Roman times. No trace is now left of this south wall, but the others do exist in much ruined and fragmentary form, often moved bodily several metres from their original positions by landslips.

The walls are 3·50 m thick and composed of the usual rubble concrete with a facing each side of Kentish ragstone and tile-courses. At the base there is a simple offset course of facing stones on both interior and exterior, without a trace of the usual pebble foundation. The interior rubble is set in a hard white mortar, composed of lime, sand and pebbles, but the facing stones are surrounded by a much finer mortar, which also includes pounded tile.

Fig. 34 Drawing of the east gate at Lympne, excavated in
the mid-nineteenth century.

Fig. 35 The east gate of the fort of Lympne as excavated in 1976. Since the
nineteenth-century excavations, the right-hand tower has disappeared,
but otherwise the gate's condition seems to be little altered.

There are external towers at intervals, all, except one, bonded into the wall. They project 4·5 m and are semicircular. The exception appears to have cracked away from the wall because of earth movement, but even so the tile-courses in it are spaced differently from those in the wall next to it. One of the towers on the west side has an internal room at ground level with the marks of wooden shuttering in the mass of concrete rubble which forms the roof.

There is at least one postern gate, defended by one of the flanking towers, but the main gate appears to have lain in the south-east corner. Engravings of the gate as excavated in the 1850s show it in a much ruined state (Fig. 34) as a result of the land movements to which the site is subject. Re-excavation of this gate (Fig. 35) in 1976, as part of a campaign of research at the site by Professor Barry Cunliffe, showed the general accuracy of the Victorian excavators' observations, but showed that landslides had left the remains of the gate in a far more complicated state than they had suspected. Careful analysis of the remains showed not only that their gate plan (shown on Fig. 33) was totally erroneous, but that the gate could be reconstructed as a normal simple portalled entrance flanked by a pair of semi-circular towers.

Professor Cunliffe's excavations at the foot of the hill have also revealed that the south wall has slumped considerably into the marsh. Because it is difficult to tell how much slipping of the walls has occurred since Roman times, even the original shape of the wall-circuit is not known.

Interior buildings have been found, at a great depth and much disturbed. In the northern part of the fort, broken walls indicate that there was once a row of buildings across the central area; a building measuring 10 by 40 m was found towards the middle of this range. The baths have also been located, lying in the south-east corner of the fort.

The second-century altar of a commander of the British fleet, Aufidius Pantera (*RIB* 66), found reused in the gate-platform, shows that Lympne had contacts with the *Classis Britannica* before the mid second century, and there still remain to be found somewhere the sites not only of the harbour, but also of the base of the earlier fleet. Possibly the earlier fort was in a different place from that occupied by the Saxon Shore fort, for the barnacle-encrusted altar attests a period of disuse of the site; but there also remains the possibility that the buildings found within the fort, because of their great depth, belong to an earlier phase of occupation, as do the *Classis Britannica* tiles found here reused in a late third-century context. Inside the Saxon Shore fort itself, nothing is known of any occupation-layers: coin-finds suggest that the main use of the fort was in the late third century, and also under Constantine in the early fourth century. No coins of later date than 367 have been found.

Pevensey

The walls of the Saxon Shore fort enclose a rough oval promontory of slightly higher ground amid surrounding marshes. The site is linked to the mainland by a road from the west which enters the fort by the main gate; smaller gates on the north and east suggest there may have been other tracks giving access to the fort across the marshes. The site of the harbour is not known, but Pevensey obviously commanded a marshy estuary in Roman times.

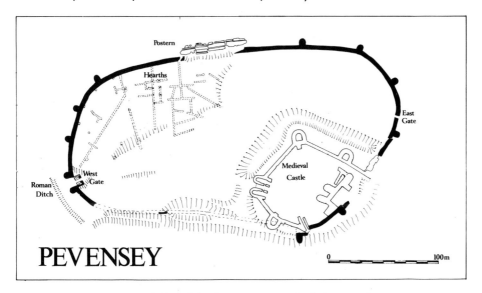

Fig. 36 Plan of the fort at Pevensey. Scale 1:3333.

The construction of the walls was begun by the excavation of a foundation trench 4·50 m wide, with the upcast on the inside of the fort. Into the bottom of this trench were driven oak piles, and around them a layer of flints and clay approximately 0·60 m thick was packed, then above this another layer of flints and chalk 0·50–1·00 m thick, on the top of which a framework of beams set in a criss-cross pattern was placed (Fig. 75, p. 142), to give added cohesion to the foundation courses and to ensure that the bastions were bonded well with the wall at the lowest level. Above this, a further 0·20 m of mortar was spread, then two courses of medium sized stones forming a plinth upon which the wall, 3·70 m thick, was itself constructed in a fashion similar to those of all the other forts. The core was built of flint and concrete rubble, faced with cubes of small ashlar masonry, which is composed partly of dark brown ironstone and partly of green sandstone. At about 2·50 m from ground level on the inside face there is one offset, but the wall appears to have had a width of 3·50 m or so for its full height, which was at least 8 m; above that level there was a

Fig. 37 View of the north wall of the fort at Pevensey, showing a
tower still preserving a Roman window at rampart-walk height.
This picture was taken in 1932: the insertion of a machine-gun
post in the tower in 1939–40 obliterated this window.

string course and battlements. Tile-courses appear in the outer face of the wall
at intervals, but are very irregular, and in some parts of the wall are not found
at all; bonding courses of larger flat stone slabs as in the walls of Silchester
were used when tiles were lacking.

Eleven large U-shaped bastions are now visible round the walls, all of one
build with the wall, as both the facing stones and the plan of the timber beams
underneath them show, since the beams are there partly to tie in the bastions
to the wall core. These bastions are 5 m in diameter and project 6 m from the
wall. Along the long straight north and south sides of the fort there are traces
of a few bastions, though much of the walls in these parts has fallen. The
bastions are concentrated in particular on the curved parts of the encircling
wall, and vary between 25 and 40 m apart. Clearly they were positioned so as
to provide cover for the walls, but were not felt to be so necessary on the long
straight stretches. Originally their windows were large and U-shaped (Fig. 37).

Three gates are known: the east gate is a simple archway 3 m wide, with the
nearest bastion to the south 12 m away. No guard-chambers were discovered
on excavation. A postern gate on the north side, approximately 1·50 m wide,
and vaulted with a curved tile roof, ran obliquely and on a curving path
through the wall. The main gate, on the west, lay set back between a pair of
bastions which formed an entrance 10 m wide by 6 m deep. Behind this, their
front walls flush with the interior face of the main wall, are two guard-
chambers containing rooms 3·30 by 1·50 m, with a passageway 3 m wide
between them. Underneath and between the gate-towers, excavations in the

1930s found that the chalk and flint foundation with the timber beams laid on it continued round the full circuit (Fig. 68, p. 124).

The wall of the fort is built in sections. A complete picture of which gangs built which parts, and the lengths of walling assigned to the various gangs for building, cannot be accurately provided, since about a third of the total circuit has fallen; but it is clear that all the walls now standing have been built by at least four different gangs of builders. Building lengths differ widely, but for the most part it appears that a particular gang was given a length of about 20 m or so to build, usually incorporating one bastion and a length of curtain walling. Distinctive styles—the use of bands of ironstone, or the presence of differing numbers of tile-courses—betray the work of one gang or another. But the presence of various types of wall-facing at different points round the circuit prompts questions about how the work thus apportioned was organized. Because of the construction method it would not be possible to have a finished piece of wall next to one which had not been started. So perhaps all that the 'distinctive styles' of wall-building shows is that there were several gangs working, and that the supply and availability of a particular sort of building material at any particular time in the construction of the fort might vary. The building-sections in the walls have been compared in style, size, and length with those of the walls at Richborough, but since so much depended on the availability of the right material at the right time, it follows that, for instance, the 'distinctive band of ironstone' normally seen as the particular mark of one or another building gang at both sites, may be merely an accidental occurrence.

Surprisingly little trace has ever been found of interior buildings; but in 1906–8 Salzman found a series of tiled hearths, perhaps from wooden barrack-blocks, set regularly at 6 m intervals, and also a timber-lined well. But no coherent pottery group has been published, though perhaps that would have gone a long way towards solving the vexed problem of the date of construction and occupation of the fort. Bushe-Fox found a coin of Constantinian date (335) in one of the beam holes underneath one of the external towers, and in his mention of it he asks how the coin could have got 3–4 feet underneath the masonry even if the end of the hole had been open, except by being dropped there at the time of building. Excavations later in the 1930s showed that the initial occupation layers of the fort contained large amounts of late third-century pottery and Carausian coins. Part of the ditch to the west of the fort was cleared, and the earliest find from it was a piece of second-century pottery. At some stage in the later fourth century, a roadway was built across the ditch using the large blocks from the south-west guardhouse which accordingly must already have been in disrepair. But no structures at all were found in the centre of the fort, even though much of the central area consists of a large clay dump, presumably dug out of the moat of the Norman castle. Possibly an earlier site existed somewhere nearby, since *CLBR* tiles have been found, though not in the walls of the fort. Tiles with the rare stamp *HON AUG ANDRIA*, usually taken to signify *Honorius Augustus Anderida*, have also been found; these were thought to show that the fort was still in occupation at the end of the fourth century. But it now appears that these tiles, which are of a deep blue-black colour, and of which only the stamped parts have been discovered, are forgeries probably perpetuated by Charles Dawson, who 'found' the original stamp of which Salzman discovered a broken example at a depth of 2 feet 4 in in his excavations in the 1900s (see Fig. 78 and p. 147).

Portchester

The topography of the surroundings of Portchester, set at sea-level deep inside Portsmouth Harbour, cannot have changed much since Roman times. The Isle of Wight has protected the flat, marshy ground between the Solent and Chichester from being swept away by strong currents prevailing from the south-west and so a series of accessible harbours below the ridge of chalk downs still survives in the area. One side of the fort is virtually washed by the sea; the other sides are protected by ditches which closely encircle the site.

The fort is nearly square and encloses almost four hectares. Its walls, built of rubble concrete with tile-courses, though much rebuilt and patched in medieval times, are still very impressive, but are only 6 m high, in contrast with Pevensey's 8 m. At this height there still exists a wall-walk and parapet, but these may be medieval. Along much of the wall's length, the original Roman thickness, some 4 m, has been reduced in medieval times to approximately half this width, with the result that at various points on the interior face of the wall one can see clearly the layering of flints and mortar in the core of the wall.

Frequent external towers punctuate the wall-face. They are hollow and U-shaped and would have numbered twenty in all, spaced at regular intervals of 30 m. From one excavated base on the west side it is shown that their foundations were square and timber framed and that the hollow U-shaped part above ground was built above this square base. One of the missing towers on the east side was covered with sea gravel, showing that once the sea did actually lap up against the walls of the fort and may have caused the collapse of towers on that side. Lacing-courses of tile and stone tend to be more frequent in the tower facings than in the wall.

The gates are four in number—two posterns, simple entrances, 3·30 m wide, to the north and south, and two main gateways set centrally east and west. Both of these last are of unusual plan, but are paralleled, and perhaps developed, by those at Pevensey (Fig. 66, p. 121). The wall, on approaching the gateway, turns through 90 degrees, and runs inwards into the fort a

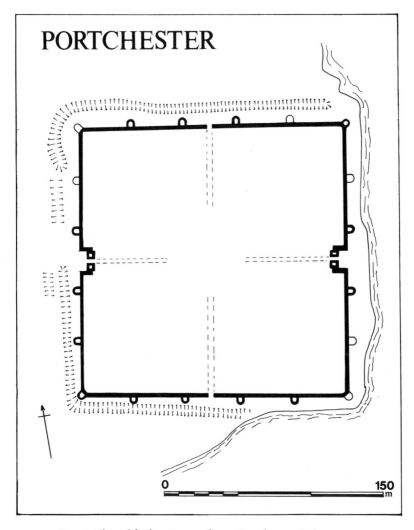

Fig. 38 Plan of the late Roman fort at Portchester. Scale 1:2500.

distance of 11 m, forming a rectangular entrance courtyard, 11 m by 14 m, at the back of which two guard-towers are set, narrowing the entrance further to only 3·30 m and commanding the roadway. The arrangement is similar to that at Pevensey, but at Portchester there are no semicircular towers projecting at the opening of this enfiladed gateway, and the only towers in the vicinity are those set at the normal distance along the curtain wall. Both the Watergate and the Landgate have this plan, which is unparalleled elsewhere on the Saxon Shore.

The walls are built in sections: levelling courses of 'dead men'—stones put in to ensure the right correspondence between building sections—have been noted at different points on the wall circuit, and they seem to occur about 1 m south of the towers on the west side, giving a building length of approximately 30 m for each wall-section. The whole of the wall is based on timber beams, as in many of the other forts, and it has been established that, after digging the foundation trench of the walls, the builders used the earth so displaced to level off the fort platform.

Despite the fact that much of the site had been disturbed by periods of occupation and cultivation in post-Roman times in an almost unbroken sequence up to the present day, there were some traces of Roman timber buildings, wells, pits and streets. The construction phases of this fort are dated after 261 by finds of coins in foundation-levels, and the next stage of organization of the interior of the fort, the levelling of the ground, which involved piling earth against the inside of the wall, is dated after 286–7 because of the discovery of Carausian coins in the material so used. Apart from these definite dated instances, information about the use of the site in the later Roman period is mainly derived from the groups of pottery found associated in wells or pits, and from the relative frequency or scarcity of coin-finds of any particular period.

The coin-finds from Professor Cunliffe's excavation at the site show a number of possible phases of activity or inactivity at the fort. A substantial number of coins dating from the early Carausian period (A.D. 285–90) were found, but during the decade 290–300 there were very few coins from the site, when compared with the same period at other sites within Britain. Then followed a period, from 300–17, when Portchester had an abnormally high percentage of coins recovered from the excavation, and this was followed by a time during which there were some fluctuations in the numbers of coins found, but revealing no substantial differences from the British norm from other comparable sites. From 345, however, until 364, there is again an abnormally low number of coins at the site, but after that date, the finds reach once again what is about the British norm, a pattern followed almost to the end of the fourth century.

It is an open question whether the numbers of coins lost at any particular period are an adequate indication of the scale of occupation at that period. The Roman army was a great user of coin for the payment of the troops' salaries, and there is therefore good reason to suppose that the periods when substantial numbers of coins were finding their way to the site and then being lost (one must suppose that coin-finds from excavations represent coins 'lost' in antiquity) were those of military occupation. It could be argued, however, that the periods when few coins were being lost were also those of occupation of a careful and tidy kind: this might also suggest the presence of a disciplined body of men.

It is not realistically possible to postulate a definite end to military occupation at Portchester in about A.D. 370. Coin-loss at the site continued until the early 380s, with a possible break in occupation soon after. That this period was combined with a rather more squalid phase of occupation of the interior of the fort itself perhaps suggests, but in no way proves, that the military by now had little hold on the site. The earlier phases of use of the site had on the whole been tidier: rubbish was then not allowed to pile up, and although the excavations failed to locate any regular arrangement of timber barrack-blocks, something of the sort must have lain within the walled area.

One particularly interesting aspect is the evidence for post-Roman occupation of the site. Some form of occupation continued up until the very end of the fourth century. The first finds after that date are huts of Saxon *Grubenhaus* type, which suggest fifth-century—possibly even early fifth-century—German settlements within the walled area. In addition, a Roman timber well, which had earlier fallen into disuse, was redug and relined with a new timber revetment. A fairly continuous occupation sequence is therefore established, and this possibly was not broken by much more than fifty years during the Roman and sub-Roman periods.

4 THE *NOTITIA*

The system of Shore forts itself is mentioned in only a single Roman source, the *Notitia Dignitatum*, a document of unique value for later Roman military history. It is a list (surviving only in illustrated manuscript copies of the fifteenth and later centuries) comprising all important late Roman civil and military officials, under whose names appear the provinces and areas over which they held command; the list gives military appointments and postings in great detail. Thus, for wide parts of the Roman empire in its later stages, there exist precise records not only of the disposition of forts, but also of the names of units which were stationed at them. Fort-names which the *Notitia* provides can in many cases be linked to remains on the ground: occasionally a name from the *Notitia* identifies a place, where remains no longer survive, as a Roman fort.

Information in the *Notitia* about the positioning of garrisons cannot always be contemporaneously valid, since there are cases where what appears to be the same body of troops is found at two different forts. Not only does the *Notitia* comprise lists of forts and their commanding officers, but also registers of the units of the field army. This was a mobile reserve, quite separate from, and apparently superior in status to, the static troops in the defended posts. Some units listed seem to be recorded in two places—both as a frontier command and in the field army. Although a garrison was removed from one fort to another, or transferred into the higher grade mobile reserve, its name and position were retained in the *Notitia* for both its old and new situations.

The *Notitia* is thus a notoriously difficult document to use: it contains material which we can recognize as applicable to different dates within the late Roman period, and therefore its efficiency as a working handbook (if this is what it was) for contemporary officials must have been impaired. Nevertheless, the manuscript which has come down to us is probably a copy of a late Roman handbook, in which the basic information is relatively accurate for *c.* A.D. 395, and to which additions have been made to keep parts of it at least up to date until about 430. The document lists both halves of the empire separately, with the western half, as far as can be judged, rather more fully kept up to date with current troop movements: the copy which we have is therefore likely to have been in use in the western half of the empire; information about the eastern half is included for reference.[1]

Of particular interest is one of the chapters of the western half of the *Notitia* which deals with the office of the *Comes Litoris Saxonici*, the 'Count of the Saxon Shore'. It lists his official staff and the commanders of troops with their

Fig. 39 The insignia of the *Comes Litoris Saxonici per Britannias* from the Oxford *Notitia* manuscript (Canon misc. 378b, Bodleian Library).

postings under his authority. It is thus a contemporary record of the forts and garrisons which formed the *Litus Saxonicum*, the 'Saxon Shore'. Its uniqueness lies in the fact that it is the only source which mentions this name for the system of fortifications round the south and east coasts. The chapter (28) deserves quotation in full (see also Fig. 39):

Sub dispositione viri spectabilis Comitis Litoris Saxonici per Britanniam
    Praepositus numeri Fortensium, Othonae
    Praepositus militum Tungrecanorum, Dubris
    Praepositus numeri Turnacensium, Lemannis
    Praepositus equitum Dalmatarum Branodunensium, Branoduno
    Praepositus equitum Stablesianorum Gariannonensium, Gariannonor
    Tribunus cohortis primae Baetasiorum, Regulbio

Praefectus legionis secundae Augustae, Rutupis
Praepositus numeri Abulcorum, Anderidos
Praepositus numeri exploratorum, Portum Adurni [2]

Under the command of his excellency, the Count of the Saxon Shore
    The commander of the unit of Fortenses, at Othona
    The commander of the Tungrecanian troops, at Dubrae
    The commander of the unit of Turnacenses, at Lemannis
    The commander of the Branodunensian Dalmatian cavalry, at Branodunum
    The commander of the Gariannonensian Stablesian cavalry, at Gar-
riannon(um?)
    The tribune of the first Baetasian cohort, at Regulbium
    The prefect of the second legion, the Augusta, at Rutupae
    The commander of the unit of Abulci, at Anderid(a?)
    The commander of the unit of scouts (*exploratores*) at (or to?) Portus Adurni

Under the list of the Count's forts and their garrisons comes the group of clerical staff permanently attached to the office. Nine forts, then, are listed under the control of the Count; in order to understand the system, we need to discover how these names tally with the late Roman forts which are known from their archaeological remains along the southern and eastern coastline (Fig. 40).

Such a marriage of written and archaeological evidence is not always easy: we must remember that the *Notitia* survives only as a fifteenth-century copy of a manuscript which must have had its origins at the end of the fourth century. There may be many copyist's errors, particularly in names, which are usually unfamiliar words, but from comparison with other documents of Roman original date (for example Itineraries which list stopping points along major routes)[3] it is possible to identify some of the forts here listed with some degree of certainty.

Among the most obvious are *Dubris* and *Rutupis*, which are known from other sources to be the channel ports of Dover and Richborough respectively. Because of their focal position for the Channel crossing, they occur regularly enough in the Itineraries. *Lemannis*, the third Channel port, can be identified as Lympne in Kent, both from mentions in other sources and from the fact that there is a Roman fort of Saxon Shore type there. *Regulbium* is Reculver, for the same reasons. *Anderidos* refers to Pevensey, which in late Saxon times was known as 'Andreadsceaster'; the identification is strengthened by the further evidence of the Ravenna Cosmography, which places *Anderelio* in the south of England. The East Anglian sites are represented by *Gariannonum*, which must have been at the mouth of the *Gariennus* river mentioned by Ptolemy.

Burgh Castle stands near the Waveney estuary, on the River Yare, which could easily be a derivative of the Latin *Gariennus*: Brancaster still preserves

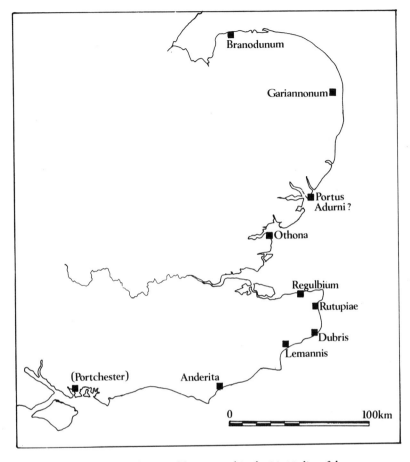

Fig. 40 The placing of forts named in the *Notitia* list of the
Comes Litoris Saxonici per Britannias.

the name and meaning of *Branodunum*, a Latinized Celtic name meaning
'Camp of Branos', as well as again providing ample evidence that there was a
Roman fort on the site.

The only two names which are difficult to identify are *Othona* and *Portus
Adurni*. *Othona* is most likely to be Bradwell, on the Blackwater estuary,
which has some remains of a Roman fort of Saxon Shore type. Bede, when he
wrote his history of the English Church, mentioned a town of Saxon date
which must have been sited on or very near the site of the Roman fort at
Bradwell.[4] He called the name of the place 'Ythancaestir', on the River
'Pent'. Undoubtedly Bede meant to refer to Bradwell by this name, but the
derivation of 'Ythancaestir' from *Othona* is not accepted by all philologists.
But the spelling of names in the *Notitia*, as well as in manuscripts of Bede, may
have become distorted through copyists' errors in the manuscripts, and what

is now philologically unacceptable may only be the result of poor scribal transmission.

If, then, *Othona* is Bradwell, the remaining name to be assigned to a site is *Portus Adurni*. It is in attempting to relate this name to one of the forts attested by archaeological remains along the channel coast that we find the evidence of the *Notitia* at its most intractable. Unfortunately, though eight names have been assigned easily enough to forts which have left some traces, there are still at least two other forts of late Roman date known along the south and east coastline of Britain. Both Portchester and Walton Castle have some claim to the name of *Portus Adurni*, and to inclusion in the scheme of Channel defence under the command of the Count of the Saxon Shore.

In fact, there is no reason to suppose that both forts were not part of the Channel defence system. This is where the date of the *Notitia* list becomes all-important: the fact that there are only nine names in the *Notitia*, but at least ten forts attested by the archaeological remains, may only mean that at the time when the *Notitia* list was written down, only nine forts were in use. The tenth, whichever it was, may by then have been either totally abandoned or temporarily vacant, and therefore not on the list (since only commanders of garrisoned forts appear), or else not yet built. All depends on the *Notitia*: what date is the information given in the chapter about the Saxon Shore? Does it represent a simple picture of the strength and garrisons of the Saxon Shore at one given moment in the later years of the Roman empire, or is it a composite picture of fragments of information sent in at various times?

Unfortunately, also, archaeology cannot help. Walton Castle will never be dated by archaeological means, as the only evidence for its date is a rather scant coin-series from the fort site and its neighbouring region which presents much the same picture for Roman occupation as the other forts along the east coast. We do know, however, that the whole site was still standing in the seventeenth century, and that it was therefore usable as a fort right up to the end of the Roman period need not be doubted. Portchester, too, even though part of the fort site has been thoroughly excavated, presents some problems: although there are relatively scant traces of occupation from about 370 onwards, we cannot assume that troops were not in garrison there after that date. Thus, though it has in the past been argued that Portchester could not be listed in the *Notitia* because it had no garrison at the time that that document was written down (in the last years of the fourth century) this is no longer necessarily a valid claim.

The name *Portus Adurni* may give a further clue. If we assume that *Adurnus* was the name of the river on whose estuary the port stood (as did the nineteenth-century antiquarians who named a south-coast river the Adur to support their claim that the Roman site lay near Portslade)[5] then this might suggest that the identification of Portchester with the name *Portus Adurni* is incorrect. Portchester, almost uniquely of the Saxon Shore forts, is not sited on a river estuary, but on the inland reach of tidal water round Portsmouth. But there is no confirmation that Adurnus need be the name or a river: admittedly there were at Lympne, Dover, and Burgh Castle respectively rivers called the *Lemannis, Dubris,* and *Gariennus*: but other *Portus* names in the *Notitia* cannot be demonstrably proved to have been in all cases formed from river-names.

Arguments in the past about the identification of *Portus Adurni* have centred on the information given in the *Notitia* about troops stationed at other forts in Britain. The garrison of *Portus Adurni* is the *numerus exploratorum*, 'the unit of scouts', which is commonly supposed to have been the same unit of troops which was formerly stationed in the fort at Netherby, north of Hadrian's Wall. This fort was abandoned in 367–9,[6] if it had not already been so in 342.[7] But *numeri exploratorum* arc common enough in the *Notitia* throughout the empire, and a more likely fort to have received the former garrison of Netherby would be the fort at Bowes (*Lavatrae*), which has a garrison of the same name figuring in the *Notitia* list of forts in northern Britain.[8] It cannot be certain therefore that the garrison of *exploratores* at *Portus Adurni* is the one from Netherby, having moved south after a collapse and rebuilding of Hadrian's Wall in 367–9.

Better evidence for an overall date later than 369 for the *Notitia* list of Saxon Shore forts comes from the other forts and their garrisons. Three of them, the *Equites Dalmatarum Branodunensium*, the *Equites Stablesianorum Gariannonensium*, and the *Cohors I Baetasiorum* were troop units which had been in their position for some time in the forts in which they are listed. The first two include the placename in their title, implying that the unit had had time enough to become definitely linked to the fort; the third unit is a cohort.[9] Tiles from Reculver stamped *CIB* and referring to this unit of troops have been found in recent excavations, and from their context show that the unit had been stationed there since the early years of the third century. A further indication that the troops had never moved is the survival of the name 'cohort', which signified a unit of an older style. If the troops had ever been transferred, they might have changed their name and formation.

A fourth unit, the *Legio Secunda Augusta* at Richborough, had been in Britain since the earliest days of the Roman conquest. It had been stationed at Caerleon (*Isca*) until the latest years of the third century, when it was probably transferred to Richborough on the Saxon Shore.[10] This probably remained the home base of the legion until the abandonment of Britain, although detachments of it were no doubt sent to serve in the field army while leaving the *Praefectus* at headquarters.[11]

The *Tungrecani* at Dover may have been brought into Britain by Theodosius at the time of the restoration of the province in 369. The name of the unit shows that they had originally come from Tongres or from its surrounding territory in *Germania Secunda*. The name is a relatively common one, however, and may refer to a body of troops raised from among the *Tungri*, rather than being one which had grown, like that of the *Equites Gariannonenses*, from service at a particular fort site in 'Tungrian' territory. *Tungrecani* appear both in the field army and among the frontier troops elsewhere and may in some cases be referring to earlier or later postings of the same unit as is listed for the Saxon Shore. From other sources, we learn of the presence of troops of the same name in Switzerland (*Maxima Sequanorum*)[12] and in the eastern empire in 365.[13] There was a unit also at a battle near Châlon-sur-Saône in 367.[14] Any one of these units may have been the one which later came to Dover.

The *Turnacenses* at Lympne provide a roughly parallel case. Their name is also unmistakably a geographical name rather than a title and must mean that originally the troops were connected with Tournai, a small town near Tongres, but in *Gallia Belgica*. When the security of Britain was threatened by barbarians in 367, Theodosius may have collected some of the nearest units of troops from northern Gaul, on his way to answer the emergency: later, these units stayed, to strengthen the Shore forts or to replace lost garrisons.[15]

The best evidence of a late date for the chapter on the Saxon Shore is provided by Pevensey. The fort's name was *Anderetia*, or *Anderida*, and the occurrence of two units bearing a similar name in the *Notitia* shows that the Saxon Shore chapter was late enough for substantial changes to have been made in the fort garrisons from their original forces. The *milites Anderetianorum* are found at *Vicus Julius*, in the command of the *Dux Mogontacensis*,[16] and the *Classis Anderetianorum* is found at Paris.[17] Both these units must originally have been at Pevensey, and have been moved at some later time to the positions they hold in the *Notitia* lists.

The garrison of Pevensey, as given in the *Notitia*, is the *numerus Abulcorum*. Detachments of *Abulci* are known from other sources in the later empire: they were involved in the defeat of Magnentius at Mursa, in *Pannonia Secunda* (now Yugoslavia) in 351,[18] and it is evident here from Zosimus that they were at the time considered to be a crack unit of troops. A body of men of the same name also occurs in the list of the field army in Gaul.[19] Whether this was originally a geographical or even functional name is not certain, but its comparative rarity suggests that, in all three cases, the same body of troops is referred to: in particular, the troops named among the army at Mursa are likely to have been the same unit which was later transferred to the west. The garrison of Pevensey need only be a comparatively small detachment from the main body in the field army.

Little is known of the garrison of *Othona*, the *Fortenses*. A legion, part of the field army in the western empire, was called by the same name, and it is recorded, possibly at some later date, in Spain.[20] Another legion of the same name is known from Africa. No doubt these two legions provided all the garrisons of this name at those forts which held them.

It is interesting that the whole chapter is headed by a *Comes*, 'Count', rather than a *Dux*, 'General'. This is unusual, as the chapter stands, since *Comites* were more normally in charge of the field army from the late fourth century onwards rather than of frontier troops, who were in general state.[21] That the post of *Comes Litoris Saxonici* once held control over a larger area than is described in the British chapter in the *Notitia* is shown by the fact that two forts which lay on the Continental shore are also specifically described as being *in Litore Saxonico*, 'on the Saxon Shore'. They lie in the territory and under the command of two Continental commanders, the *Dux Belgicae Secundae* (the Duke, or General of Belgica Secunda) and the *Dux Tractus Armoricani* (the General of the Armorican region).[22] For further discussion of these sites see pp. 89–95.

By the time that the *Notitia* list of the Saxon Shore garrisons had been written, the original extent of the command had been curtailed. Although a *Comes*, and therefore entitled to command troops of a higher grade, its commander was reduced to being in charge only of static frontier garrisons. Despite his higher rank, he had fewer forts under his control than, for example, the *Dux Britanniarum* (the General of the British provinces), who held control of Hadrian's Wall and the northern British forts. This, with all the other evidence for movements of the troop units which make up the garrisons of the forts, suggests that a date well after the reorganization of Britain's defence in 369 is likely for this chapter. It probably represents the state of the Saxon Shore forts in or around A.D. 395 (see pp. 148–50).

If this is so, then at this date Portchester is unlikely to have been represented as *Portus Adurni* and despite the lack of evidence about Walton's period of occupation, the name may be assigned to the latter.[23] Walton is in an ideal position for a Saxon Shore fort, standing near the mouth of three rivers, any one of which may have had a safe harbour.

Even in this interpretation there are problems. The published series of coin-finds from Lympne (*Lemannis*) stops at 369. This has prompted the view that the fort was vacant after that date, and as Lympne quite definitely does appear in the *Notitia* list, it has been argued that the whole list dates from earlier than 367 and represents the state of affairs before the crisis and rearrangement of 368–9.[24] It is then possible that Portchester is *Portus Adurni*? Although it cannot be conclusively proved, there are indications in the *Notitia* that the list is actually of a later date, and there is no other historical context as likely for the rearrangements which we seem to see as a *fait accompli* indications in the *Notitia* pages as the events of 367–9. The evidence from Lympne of an abandonment can hardly be trusted implicitly, since the site has not been touched by excavation since 1895, and evidence for abandonment, whether at Lympne or Portchester, has to be established by the positive lack of later finds, not by the comparative lack of any finds from an unexcavated site.

Finally, although the *Notitia* gives us the name 'Saxon Shore', it fails to give any precise date when the term can be applied. All that can be said is that at the time when the *Notitia* was written, the name was well established for this area of the empire, though the date of inception of the name *Litus Saxonicum*, while it predates the *Notitia* list and refers to a time when both sides of the Channel were united under one command, cannot be determined. As there is no strict definition of the term, modern usage has also become slack, and refers it to the coastal defence system at any time in the late third or the fourth century. It is possible that the name dates from the end of the third century, or even that the coastline had been known for even longer as the 'Saxon Shore'. For the discussion of the date of the term, and its precise significance, see pp. 147f.

Perhaps the most important piece of information about the Saxon Shore to be gleaned from the pages of the *Notitia* is the fact that the *Comes Litoris Saxonici* was in charge of a *limes*, or frontier.[25] This post is listed together with other Counts and Generals in the *Notitia* specifically as a frontier command. This, though perhaps many times assumed in the past, has not up till now been given the significance which it deserves. Where there is a frontier, a *limes*, the Romans would have understood there to be a distinct fortified line. The Saxon Shore was the only maritime frontier in the whole of the Roman empire: tactics and strategy of the land-based frontiers of the empire have been worked out and discussed many times, but never for the set of unique circumstances which formed a frontier out of a series of strong forts set on small river estuaries. Only by appreciating this series of defences as a frontier system can we judge its working, and assess the Roman genius in using it to control the seas for so long.

5 CONTINENTAL COMPARISON

The major ancient source for our knowledge of the Continental defensive arrangements is, as in Britain, the *Notitia Dignitatum*, of which the relevant portions dealing with the Channel coast are chapters 37 and 38 of the western section of the list. Chapter 37 runs thus (see also Fig. 41):

Fig. 41 The insignia of the *Dux Tractus Armoricani* from the Oxford text of the *Notitia*.

Sub dispositione viri spectabilis Ducis Tractus Armoricani et Nervicani:
> *Tribunus cohortis primae novae Armoricanae, Grannona in Litore Saxonico*
> *Praefectus militum Carronensium, Blabia*
> *Praefectus militum Maurorum Benetorum, Benetis*
> *Praefectus militum Maurorum Osismiacorum, Osismis*
> *Praefectus militum Superventorum, Mannatias*
> *Praefectus militum Martensium, Aleto*
> *Praefectus militum Primae Flaviae, Constantia*
> *Praefectus militum Ursariensium, Rotomago*
> *Praefectus militum Dalmatarum, Abrincatis*
> *Praefectus militum Grannonensium, Grannono*

Extenditur tamen Tractus Armoricani et Nervicani limitis per provincias quinque:
> *per Aquitanicam Primam*
> *et Secundam*
> *Lugdunensem Senoniam*
> *Secundam Lugdunensem*
> *et Tertiam*

Under the command of his excellency the Duke of the Armorican region and the Nervian frontier:
> The tribune of the first new Armorican cohort, at Grannona on the Saxon Shore
> The prefect of Carronensian troops at Blavia
> The prefect of the Venetian Moorish troops, at Venetis
> The prefect of the Osismiacan Moorish troops, at Osismi
> The prefect of reserve troops, at Mannatias (Namnetum)
> The prefect of Martenses, at Aletum
> The prefect of first Flavian soldiers, at Constantia
> The prefect of Ursariensian troops, at Rotomagus
> The prefect of Dalmatian troops at Abrincatae
> The prefect of Grannonensian troops, at Grannonum (=Grannona?)

The Duke's command extends through five provinces:
> through Aquitanica Prima and Secunda, Lugdunensis Senonia, Lugdunensis Secunda and Tertia.

Chapter 38 deals in the same way with the command of the *Dux Belgicae Secundae* (see Fig. 42):

Sub dispositione viri spectabilis Ducis Belgicae Secundae:
> *Equites Dalmatae; Marcis in Litore Saxonico*
> *Praefectus Classis Sambricae, loco Quartensi sive Hornensi*
> *Tribunus militum Nerviorum, Portu Aepatiaci*

Under the command of his excellency, the Duke of Belgica Secunda:
> The Dalmatian cavalry, at Marcae, on the Saxon Shore

The prefect of the Sambrican fleet, at the place Quartensis or Hornensis
The tribune of Nervian troops, at Portus Aepatiaci.

The archaeological remains which correspond to and amplify these lists are
sometimes very slight; but traces exist at various sites connected either directly
with the sea, or with rivers and their estuaries (Fig. 43). Of the forts under the
command of the *Dux Tractus Armoricani*, most have been identified: *Benetis* is
Vannes, known from its inclusion in a list of Gallic cities of the late fourth
century as the *Civitas Venetum*.[1] Others identifiable from the same source
include a garbled *Mannatias*, which is evidently a scribal mistake for
Namnetum,[2] Nantes. *Constantia* and *Abrincatis* both appear in the list of Gallic
cities under the province of *Lugdunensis Secunda*,[3] along with cities in the same
area such as Rouen, Lisieux and Bayeux, and are most likely to be identifiable
with Coutances and Avranches respectively, since both names clearly appear
to have an etymological link. *Rotomago*, mentioned in various spellings in
many of the ancient itinerary source-books, is well known to be Rouen. *Aleto*
is Aleth, near St Servan, a part of St Malo.

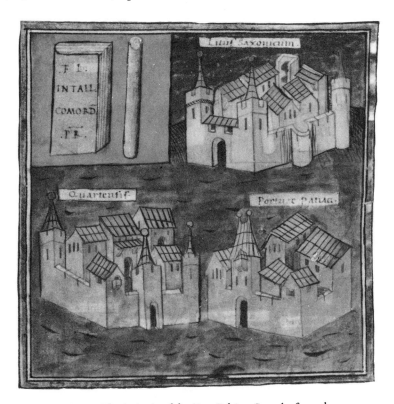

Fig. 42 The insignia of the *Dux Belgicae Secundae* from the
Oxford text of the *Notitia*.

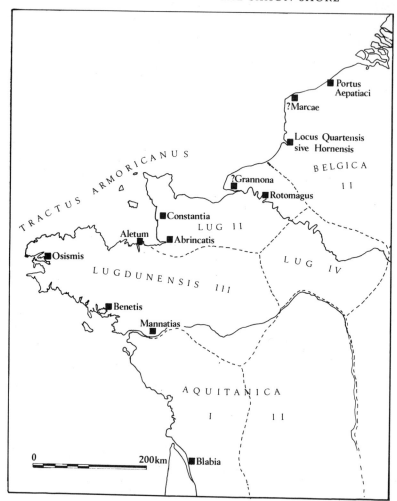

Fig. 43 The placing of forts in Gaul named in the *Notitia* lists.

The names which present difficulties are therefore *Grannona* (which appears to be repeated at the end of the list with a different garrison), *Osismis* and *Blabia*. Discussion of the siting of *Grannona* will be best left until later (pp. 93–4). *Osismis* must lie somewhere in the territory of the *Osismi*, which was in the area of the Brittany promontory: both Carhaix, thought to be the tribal capital of the *Osismi*, and Brest, where the remains of a Roman fort have been found, have been suggested. Of the two, Brest is the more likely, since it at least is on the sea and has a harbour, whereas Carhaix has none. The tribal name used alone, however, has been thought to favour decisively the identification of the site as Carhaix since only the capital of any given area would be designated in this way. Although it is admittedly unlikely, Brest could have been called *Castellum Osismorum*, or some such name, which might, for brevity, have been contracted into the form in which it appears in the *Notitia*.

Blabia is another name which on etymological grounds has been identified with several places round the western coast. It is, however, as well to bear in mind the information given in the last few lines of the *Notitia*'s entry for the *Dux Tractus Armoricani* quoted above. The area of the Duke's command spreads over five of the provinces of Gallia: *Aquitanica Prima*, of which the main centre appears to be Bourges; *Aquitanica Secunda*, the coastal area from Bordeaux to the south bank of the Loire; *Lugdunensis Tertia*, which is the area of Brittany from the Loire northwards and from Le Mans westwards; *Lugdunensis Secunda*, which includes the whole coastal area of Normandy, from the Bay of Mont St Michel eastwards at least as far as the Seine mouth and Rouen. The final area of command of the Duke is *Lugdunensis Senonia*, an inland area like *Aquitanica Prima*: it comprised the region of Paris and Sens. While the actual forts or ports under the Duke's command are in the coastal regions, it seems that it was necessary for his command to be extended to these other areas as well, possibly to control the sources of supply for his regular troops. All the sites so far mentioned have been in the two coastal *Lugdunensis* provinces, and the one large estuary where no fort has yet been placed, lying in *Aquitanica*, is that of the Garonne: *Blabia* is usually identified either with Blavet, in Brittany, or with Blaye, which lies on this estuary. On archaeological grounds, albeit very slight, the more likely of the two is Blaye: and in the Peutinger Table, dating from the late fourth century, there is a site *Blavia* nine *leugae* from Bordeaux. If this is the same site as the *Blabia* of the *Notitia*, it helps explain the inclusion of the *Aquitanica* provinces in the list of regions over which the Duke's command extended.

For the situation of *Grannona*, and the three forts named in the list of the *Dux Belgicae Secundae*, only philology has as yet given any clue. There is, however, some archaeological evidence for forts along the coastline of Gaul at places which do not appear to have been mentioned in the *Notitia* lists. This, together with evidence from those already listed and identified from the list of the *Dux Tractus Armoricani*, will be presented below: the sites will be taken from south-west to north-east, from Blaye on the Garonne to the Brittenburg north of the Rhine mouth.

Blaye

Although no trace now remains of the Roman site at Blaye, local records relate that substantial amounts of Roman material were found in the construction of the seventeenth-century fort which lay just to the north-west of the small modern town. It is probable that this platform at the water's edge was the site of *Blabia*, well positioned for a fleet-base, some way up the Garonne estuary from Bordeaux.

Nantes

The late Roman walls of Nantes are known from various excavations; they enclose a pentagonal area (Fig. 44), defended on three of its sides by the Loire and by a tributary river, the Erdre. Two sides thus faced landwards. The area enclosed is 18 hectares; the walls are 3·80 m thick along the sides defended by the rivers, but widen to 4·30 m along the two easterly facing, relatively unprotected, sides. Most of the circuit is now not visible, but a very fragmentary part remains on the eastern side, south of the cathedral, where the foundations and lowest courses of two semicircular towers can be seen.

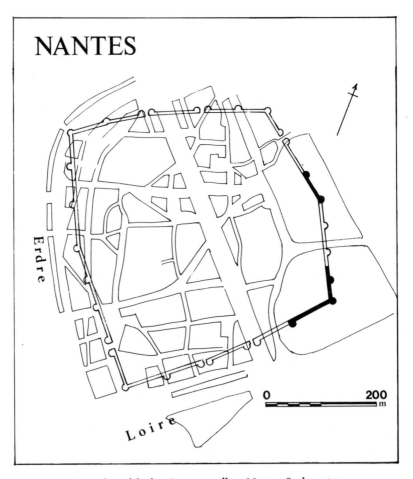

Fig. 44 Plan of the late Roman walls at Nantes. Scale 1 : 6000.

Above a single course of large stones, which includes some reused material and serves as a foundation, the superstructure is stepped back some 0·25 m. The main wall is built of blocks of *petit appareil* of local stone alternating with rows of tiles: and although it appears to vary, there are in general three rows of *petit appareil* to every triple tile-course. The tiles appear only on the outside face of the walls; the whole construction is of carefully finished workmanship.

One gate is known—though it is overlaid by the medieval gateway, the Porte St Pierre, which succeeded it. This was a single portal, flanked by two semicircular towers backed by square guard-chambers. Nearby, three more semicircular towers are known to have existed, spaced at approximately 30 m from each other; they were 7·50 m in diameter and projected 4·20 m from the wall.

Dating evidence from the walls consists in the main of reused stones in the foundation course. Two milestones have been found incorporated into the lowest levels of the walls and they date from the later years of the third century: one of Tetricus II was erected in 273, the other of Tacitus in 275. On this evidence, therefore, the *terminus post quem* for the walls of Nantes stands at 275–6.

Vannes

A roughly kite-shaped circuit of walls on a spit of land which is slightly raised above the level of the sea, and which, in Roman times, must have been much more of a promontory than it is today, was the site of the Roman *Benetis* or *Venetis* (Fig. 45). The area enclosed by the walls is approximately 5 hectares (12 acres) and the line of the defences was later followed by the medieval ramparts which still remain as one of the more impressive monuments of this town.

The Roman walls were composed of a foundation of large blocks, among which smaller stones were set to fill the gaps and declivities in the land. These blocks were levelled off to form a platform for the superstructure whose facing stones are of the usual *petit appareil* with widely-spaced tile-courses. Often, especially at the angles of the circuit, the tiles are found in single rows, but in the rest of the curtain wall they are triple and separated by up to 15 rows of *petit appareil* facing. The wall is 4 m thick, constructed of a masonry core composed of various fragments of stone and tiles set in mortar. Putlog holes have been noted in different places and are spaced 1·35 m apart horizontally and 1·50 m vertically.

Traces of towers have also been found and at least one of the medieval towers on the south-eastern portion of the ramparts stands on Roman foundations. The towers are U-shaped and project from the walls. Possibly they had a squared inside face, like their medieval successors. No dating evidence of any kind has been found, for there is a sparsity of reused material.

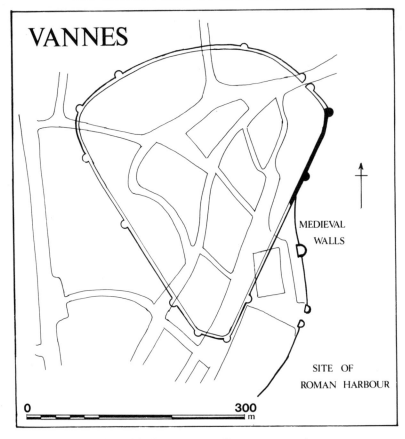

Fig. 45 Plan of the late Roman walls at Vannes. Scale 1 : 5000.

Brest

In the castle at Brest which stands on a tongue of land jutting into the harbour, fragments of Roman masonry *in situ* show that the site has a Roman origin. An outer face of walling with small blockwork and double tile-courses is visible on the landward front of the castle, which, despite additions and improvements at various dates, still retains the shape of a trapezium, which was probably the form also of the Roman fort.

The area is one of strict military security, and it has therefore not been possible to examine the site archaeologically. The north front, in which the Roman traces are most visible, is 185 m long, and was flanked in Roman times by hollow near-circular towers 6 m in diameter and 21 m apart. Though the towers were destroyed during the sixteenth and seventeenth centuries, their emplacements can still be seen from the interruptions in the Roman masonry where the towers have been pulled away from the walls. Beside one tower, there was a small postern entrance through the walls: examination of this showed that the fort wall was 4·05 m thick.

Aleth

The site is perched on a rocky promontory in the Bay of St Malo, in a position of strategic importance and defensibility—as confirmed by its choice as an emplacement for later forts and gun batteries, the latest dating from 1939 to 1945. Continuing work on the buried remains in the heart of the medieval town has shown that the site was also that of the late Roman *civitas* belonging to the tribe of the Coriosoliti. A circuit of walls, probably of Roman date, rings much of the promontory. There is also a small Roman fort, of irregular shape, which lies at the south-eastern tip of the promontory (Fig. 46) guarding the narrow neck of land which joins it to the mainland.

Excavations within the Roman fort, whose walls were later used as the medieval château, have shown from coin and pottery finds in the main levelling layers that it was first occupied in the 340s. The defended area

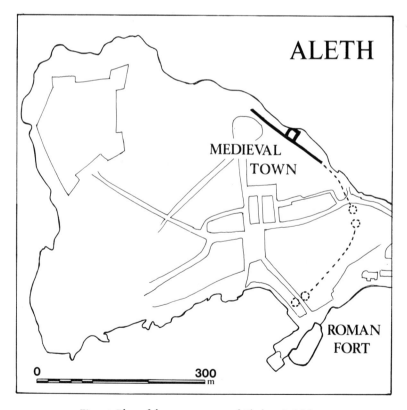

Fig. 46 Plan of the promontory of Aleth at St Malo.
Scale approx. 1:6000.

within this fort is quite tiny, and it may be that the small walled enclosure was built at this date to give extra protection to the harbour at a time when the fleet needed more bases in the western reaches of the channel.

Alderney

On Longy Bay in Alderney at the north-eastern tip of the island, there lies a small enclosure, some 40 m square, with rounded corners, usually interpreted as a Roman fortlet. The walls are 1.80 m thick, and built in part of herring-bone masonry, still standing in places to a height of 5.50 m (Fig. 47). Remains of the parapet and crenellations can be seen along parts of the wall top. Towers, either projecting from the walls or U-shaped and set astride them, are found at the corners.

There is no indication of date from finds on the site, though there are other Roman finds from the neighbourhood. The discovery of a series of wooden piles in the bay, apparently leading under the fortlet, suggests that possibly there was a landing stage here associated with the site, and its usual interpretation is as a small late post for the fleet based in the Channel to combat Saxon pirates.

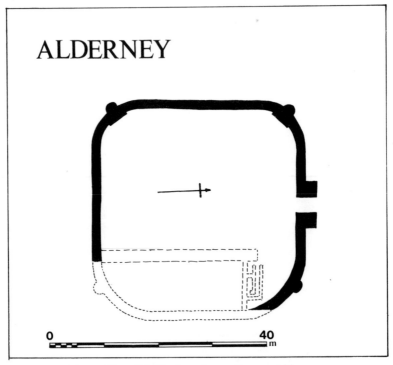

Fig. 47 Plan of the fortlet at Longy Bay, on Alderney.
Scale 1:666.

Avranches

This site appears both in the list of Gallic towns and in the list of the *Dux Tractus Armoricani*. It is set on a very high pinnacle above the surrounding countryside, with excellent views over the sea as well as over the bay in which the Mont St Michel stands. The site, some 100 m above sea-level, is too high to be closely connected with the sea or with any harbour-installations which may have existed there in Roman times, but it forms a fine look-out post and defended refuge in case of attack.

The probable course of the Roman walls was followed by the medieval circuit, parts of which are still visible round the modern town on the hill top. There is every possibility that a smaller fort, its site at the river-mouth, at present under investigation by French archaeologists, was the position of the military base.

Coutances

Like Avranches, its near neighbour Coutances stands on the top of a high hill some 90 m above sea-level, with excellent views towards the sea. Local guide-books mention the discovery of Roman walls in 1830–40, but only fragments of the medieval walls are now visible, and there is no sign of their Roman predecessors apart from a possible fragment embodied in medieval masonry east of the cathedral. Coutances is universally supposed to be the *Constantia* of the *Notitia Dignitatum*: there is a *Civitas Constantia* mentioned in the list of Gallic towns also, and this probably refers to the same place. But there is also a fort called *Constantia* lying near the mouth of the Seine, which is referred to by Ammianus Marcellinus in his brief description of Gaul (see further, p. 94).

Rouen

Buried deep under the modern town, the Roman walls of Rouen have long been sought, but only small fragments have so far been discovered. Yet the line of the walls has been thought to be responsible for the foursquare shape of the modern city. The plan published in 1907 was purely speculative, for modern discoveries have shown that much of the land between the cathedral and the River Seine is made up of mixed levels of several periods, and was reclaimed in medieval times.

A piece of walling 5 m long, found underneath the Hôtel des Finances, is a mere 1·32 m thick, but at least the outer face remains intact. It consists of *petit appareil* of limestone blocks punctuated by triple tile-courses with offsets above them. Window-like holes, found in the basement-course of the wall, were carefully faced in tiles, with tiled arches above. The remains have been interpreted as a water outlet towards the river.

Little evidence for the rest of the enceinte has been gathered: it has been variously reported that the town had four gates and that the walls were defended by square and round towers, but no real evidence for this has been found. The area reputedly enclosed by the walls is 12 hectares (30 acres), but it is much more likely to be in the region of 8 hectares (20 acres) if account is taken of the more recent findings concerning the land immediately to the south of the cathedral.

Certainly Rouen, occupying an important position on the Seine, was a busy port throughout the later Roman empire. As the chief town in the province of *Lugdunensis Secunda* it would have been an ideal situation for the headquarters of the *Dux Tractus Armoricani*; in addition, its position was convenient for a flotilla base, for the evidence of the *Notitia* makes it clear that these were increasingly located on rivers or estuaries in the later years of Roman rule.

Boulogne

Boulogne, possibly the most complex of the sites on the Continental Channel coast, has afforded more evidence than the rest for Roman occupation—as

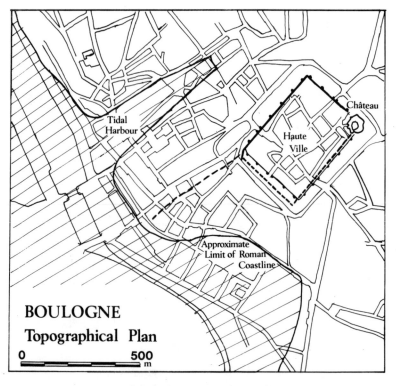

Fig. 48 General plan of Roman Boulogne, the Haute Ville
and the harbours.

befits the port which was the link with Britain throughout the 350 years of the empire. But medieval and modern Boulogne has done much to obliterate the traces of the Roman port. The once busy site of the Roman harbour has become silted up, so that it is now very difficult to determine the original configurations of the ground (Fig. 48).

The Haute Ville, on which the rectangle of medieval walls, the castle and the cathedral now stand, was defended throughout most of the Roman period. On this prominent hill not only the walls of the later imperial period—mostly deeply embedded inside the medieval circuit—but also portions of earlier Roman defences have been found. To judge from recent excavations, this portion of the town has been continuously occupied since the first century A.D.; Roman occupation of the site begins with finds of the time of Claudius. The presence of Flavian material points to continued occupation, and a series of second-century buildings, including temples and what appear to be large town-houses carries the story later still. The most recent excavations have located portions of a defensive wall which may be of second- and third-century date. After some destruction, in the later third century, the site was ringed with massive walls which, like their medieval successors, had four gateways. Those to the north-east and south-east led out into the inland areas of Gaul; the other two led to the harbour areas. These walls, enclosing an area of some 420 m by 300 m—approximately 12·6 hectares, are still to be seen in one or two places in the city, but they are buried deep within the substantial medieval ramparts of the Haute Ville.

Below the Haute Ville to the south-west a long slope (on which the modern town with all its shops now stands) stretched down to the shore area, while to the northwest an inlet of the sea formed the tidal harbour. From the Haute Ville, the Porte des Dunes gave immediate access to this harbour. Areas known to be associated with naval activity in the first and second centuries include the shore-line to the south of the Haute Ville, and it is not yet clear whether the base for the *Classis Britannica* lay in the present-day southern suburbs or whether it was connected with the second- and third-century defences found recently within the Haute Ville.

This picture is complicated by the existence of a wall, presumed to be of Roman date, which links the Haute Ville and the sea shore. It runs for some 500 m south-westwards from the south-west corner of the Haute Ville circuit, and was described early in this century. No date for this long wall has been offered, but if it is Roman then the plan and the situation indicate that it must be secondary to the main walls round the Haute Ville, and must represent a walling-off of the area between the enceinte at the top of the hill and the harbour at the shore's edge—for whatever reason.

In this short summary, the details provided by medieval sources and antiquarian writers about the walls of the Roman circuit must be curtailed.

Reports tell of walls apparently very similar to the Tour d'Odre, the Roman lighthouse, which stood to the north of the Haute Ville and was built (like the two lighthouses on the British side of the Channel) of the usual *petit appareil* facing and tile-courses (Fig. 7, p. 12). The late Roman walls round the Haute Ville were originally of the same type as those of the forts in Britain and of the neighbouring town walls on the Continent.

One of the greatest problems about Boulogne is quite separate from the difficulties over the archaeological remains. It concerns the name of the port. Three names are known for Boulogne in the ancient sources, and it has been difficult to determine whether they are all contemporary names for different parts of the town, or whether they are names applied at different times to the same occupied area. The first name is *Portus Itius*, used by Caesar in his account of the voyages to Britain in 55 and 54 B.C. Possibly this port silted up, or was abandoned early in the second century. *Gesoriacum* is the usual name for Boulogne throughout the second and third centuries, up to the usurpation of Carausius, and it is in the description of the capture of the place in 293 that the last mention is made of the *Gesoriagenses muri*, 'the walls of Gesoriacum'.[4] From then onwards the port is known only by its third name, *Bononia*. It seems possible, but probably will never be proved, that *Bononia* was renamed after the capture of Boulogne by Constantius in 293. The main problems about this theory are that the name *Bononia* appears, wherever it is found (in several places in the Roman world), to be a native name of Celtic origin. It is perhaps a little unlikely that such a name would be used in the renaming of an existing town, and in any case, a renaming to celebrate recapture by avenging Roman forces would be far more likely to honour the victor.[5] Archaeological evidence no longer allows us to argue that the Haute Ville site was first occupied only in the late third century, so the naming of that region as *Bononia* at that time does not seem to be the solution. The problem remains, as does the question, what were the *Gesoriagenses muri* which the panegyrist said were recaptured by Constantius in 293; were these the late third-century defences or was there some earlier wall? We shall be fortunate if archaeology provides answers in future campaigns of excavation at Boulogne sufficiently precise to settle the matter beyond doubt.

Oudenburg

This site, now well inland from the coastline of Belgium near Ostend, has produced the remains of a small fort of a typical late Roman plan, rectangular in shape and measuring 163 m by 146 m (Fig. 49). It stands on a slight knoll amid the surrounding flatlands, and must in Roman times have been very close to the sea's edge. The positions of all the sides of the fort have been located, as well as a large cemetery belonging to its latest phase. This contains graves

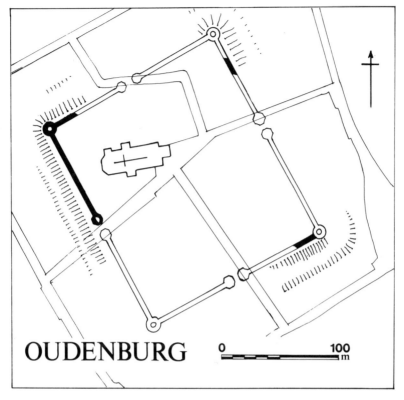

OUDENBURG

Fig. 49 Plan of the late Roman fort at Oudenburg. Scale 1:3124.

dating mainly to the last half of the fourth century, with some early in the fifth.

All that is left of the walls of the latest fort on the site are robbed foundation-trenches. It had walls 3 m thick, with round towers at the corners and polygonal towers on each side of single-portal gateways, which are set midway along each side. The fort ditch has been discovered only on the west side, but presumably also continued round the others.

The dating evidence for the fort comes from the complex stratigraphy on the west side; from the sequence of ditches outside the fort walls the excavator concluded that there were three phases of the fort's life, corresponding to three periods distinguished in the great cemetery associated with the fort. Although originally thought to belong to the late third century, the stone-built fort described above, which is the last of the three phases, is now considered to have been built in the mid or late fourth century, while the other two periods—in which the defences were of earth and timber only—have now been dated to the late third century and to the beginning of the fourth.

The BRITTENBURG

0   200 m

Fig. 50 Plan of the Brittenburg at Katwijk. Scale 1:4000.
The plan is taken from antiquarian drawings of the
Roman remains still visible on the sea-shore.

The Brittenburg

Off the coast of Holland, north of the Rhine mouth, a ruin which has now been totally swallowed by the sea is thought to have been the remains of a Roman defence for this part of the coastline. The many antiquarian records of the Brittenburg show that it was a double fortification, with a building like a granary in the central portion, and round it a strong fortified wall with projecting bastions of semicircular form. Various engravings give different plans, and on some of the drawings there are representations of double towers at the angles (Fig. 50). Such discoveries which dredging or diving at the site have produced have been mainly of second-century and early third-century date, but despite the lack of third- and fourth-century material the shape of the fortification—which is unusual for a second-century fort—suggests that it continued to be occupied, and may have been reconstructed, in the later third and fourth centuries.

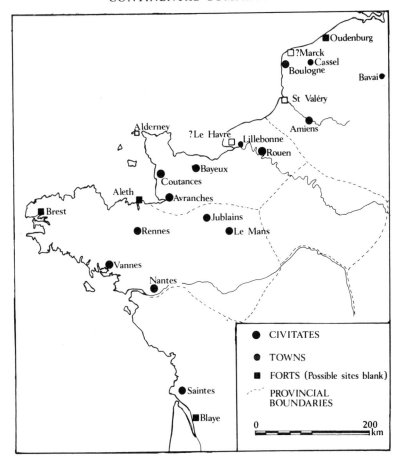

Fig. 51 Map of late Roman defences on the Channel coast
in Gaul.

From the form of the double towers at the corners, some scholars have
suggested that the later use of the site was not of late Roman, but of
Carolingian date. The central building has much in common with the well-
known shape of Roman granaries, and despite the lack of dating evidence
either of late Roman or of Carolingian date, the fortifications show that there
must have been some use of the site after the second century.

It is clear from these brief summaries that many of the sites mentioned in the
Notitia Dignitatum as being under the command of the *Dux Tractus Armoricani*
have produced remains of defences of Roman dates, however slight the traces
now may be. There was, therefore, a chain of forts around the coasts of Gaul
which could serve as bases for a fleet in the Channel, even if they were not part
of the Saxon Shore system itself (Fig. 51).

Were they part of the system, however? The *Notitia* evidence is a little ambiguous, since, of the forts under the *Dux Tractus Armoricani*, only one—*Grannona*—is specifically stated to be on the Saxon Shore; but the picture (which as usual in the *Notitia* accompanies the text and normally portrays the forts in the same order as they appear in the lists) here shows them headed, not by *Grannona*, but by *Litus Saxoniciani* in the place where *Grannona* should have appeared (Fig. 41, p. 73). Similarly, in the list of the three units of the *Dux Belgicae Secundae*, only one fort—*Marcis*—is mentioned as specifically *in Litore Saxonico*, and the picture of the three forts shows the words *Litus Saxonicum* inscribed instead of *Marcis* at the head (Fig. 42, p. 75).

Does this mean that all the forts named are in the *Litus Saxonicum* or only those two which are specifically so designated? Certainly *Marcis* and *Grannona* are two forts on the coast and at some time or other formed part of the Saxon Shore system. The rest, which do not have this description, come after *Marcis* and *Grannona*, which head their respective chapters. But the fact that *Grannona* appears to be repeated in the list of the *Dux Tractus Armoricani*, without repetition of the fort's special status, shows that the compiler had become careless about the way in which the information was recorded.

The question of the extent of the Saxon Shore in a westerly direction along the coast of Gaul depends partly on the interpretation of the term 'Saxon' and partly also on the extent of the Saxon Shore on the opposite side of the Channel, in Britain. It was argued in an earlier chapter that the system as portrayed in the *Notitia* extends from the Wash at Brancaster to Pevensey, and that of the ten known forts around the coast of Britain the one which is omitted from the list (which records nine) is that of Portchester. But though this may reflect the position which existed in the later fourth century (which must be the approximate date of the information included in the *Notitia*) it throws no light on the original extent of the *Litus Saxonicum*; Portchester and Brough-on-Humber may well have been part of the system at some earlier time. We cannot therefore say with any certainty exactly how far along the coasts of Britain the system stretched. Primarily, however, it seems to have faced eastwards: at least seven of the nine forts listed in Britain commanded an eastward-facing position. Only two—Lympne and Pevensey—are round the corner facing the Channel itself. It is improbable therefore that the Saxon Shore extended far in a westerly direction. Portchester, if ever a part of the scheme, was its westernmost limit in Britain.

This arrangement we might expect to find mirrored in Gaul. *Grannona*, which must be the more westerly of the two forts specifically placed on the *Litus Saxonicum* by the *Notitia* (since it comes under the command of the more westerly of the two officers), probably lies at some point opposite Pevensey or Portchester, or at any rate not much further west than the latter.

In Gaul, therefore, the *Litus Saxonicum* stretched into the territory

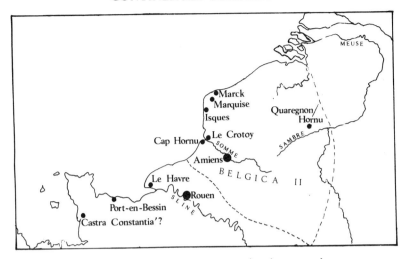

Fig. 52 Map showing sites mentioned in the text under
the discussion of the locations of *Grannona* and *Marcae*.

controlled by the *Dux Tractus Armoricani*, and came to an end inside his area of
command at some point not yet precisely defined. It must begin, by the same
token, in the territory of the *Dux Belgicae Secundae*, and must include the fort
of *Marcis*. But all three forts controlled by the *Dux Belgicae Secundae*, unlike
those further west, must lie opposite or very nearly opposite those in Britain.
In addition, all three are obviously naval bases, for despite the fact that only
Marcis is *in Litore Saxonico*—and therefore, by analogy with the British sites, a
port—the *Notitia* specifically says that at *locus* Quartensis *sive* Hornensis the
Praefectus of the *Classis Sambrica* is stationed; and though garrisoned by *milites
Nerviorum*, the third site also—*Portus Aepatiaci*—to judge from its name, is also
likely to have been a naval base, even if only for a river flotilla.

All three of the forts under the *Dux Belgicae Secundae*, therefore, could be on
the Saxon Shore. The fact that they are not so described may be because *locus
Quartensis sive Hornensis* and *Portus Aepatiaci* were newly-created forts, and
possibly belong to the period of a new arrangement, when the term *Litus
Saxonicum* was no longer applicable to Gaul. *Marcis* (and *Grannona*) originally
belonged to the earlier system, but became separated from the *Litus Saxonicum*
when the British command was separated from that of the Continent.

Unfortunately, all four of the forts in question are completely unlocated as
far as archaeological evidence is concerned (Fig. 52). *Marcis* is thought on
etymological grounds to be sited at one or other of the villages in the Pas-de-
Calais called Marck, Marquise, or Mardyck. The two former places have
yielded Roman material, and Marck, an outlying village near Calais, is
possibly the most likely candidate. The site of Mardyck was probably under

the sea in Roman times, and Marquise is not strictly on the coast but lies a little way inland from Cap Gris Nez.

Locus Quartensis sive Hornensis has been identified in two places, again on etymological grounds. One of the difficulties about this name is that we do not know the reason for the alternative apparently expressed in it: does it signify two places or one? Scholars have generally looked for a single area which might contain two places with names that could have been derived from the Roman originals. Another of the difficulties is the name of the fleet that was stationed at the fort. The text of the *Notitia* gives the name as *Classis Sambrica*, which (though the Roman name for the river is in fact unknown) has prompted some scholars to think that the fleet referred to was a river flotilla based on the Sambre, a small tributary of the Maas. Near Bavai, some 20 km north of the course of the Sambre, which is here big enough to carry canal traffic, there are two places called Quaregnon and Hornu. Both have been championed as the site of this *locus Quartensis sive Hornensis*, but neither is likely.[6] Neither is actually on the Sambre and evidence for a Roman fleet base there is extremely scanty.

A better solution is provided by emendation of the *Sambrica* of the *Notitia* to *Samarica*. The fleet thus becomes that on the River Somme. The existence of a *Classis Samarica* is suggested by the discovery in 1890 at Étaples of tiles bearing the stamp *CLSAM* (Fig. 53); a fleet of this or a similar name was stationed in

Fig. 53 Stamped tiles of the *Classis Samarica* (or *Sambrica*)
found at Étaples in the nineteenth century.

the Channel at some period. At the mouth of the Somme, near St Valéry, is a cape called Cap Hornu. Although an ideal site for a fort of the Saxon Shore type, no trace has been found of any defences; the neighbouring town of St Valéry,however, has produced some Roman material and it has an impressive circuit of medieval walls. Opposite this site, on the north side of the river mouth, is the town of Le Crotoy, which has been postulated as the etymological descendant of the Latin *Quartensis*. In addition, the presence of tiles with the *CLSAM* stamp at Étaples has been explained by supposing that the alternative expressed in *Locus Quartensis sive Hornensis* means that the *Praefectus* of the *Classis Sambrica* (*Samarica*) had alternative headquarters at two places—at Cap Hornu and at some site near Étaples, possibly the lost site of Quentovic; this had disappeared into the sea, but was a flourishing port in early medieval times. Remembering the situation at Bradwell, where a Saxon town succeeded the Saxon Shore fort, this is a likely solution. It should surely be concluded that the *Classis Sambrica* was based, not on the Sambre, but on the Somme, and that it too formed a part of the Channel defence.

Portus Aepatiaci, the third of the bases of the *Dux Belgicae Secundae*, is also unlocated. It is tempting to link it with the known site of Oudenburg, but philology gives this theory no support. Concern that Boulogne is apparently not mentioned in the *Notitia* at all has led to the suggestion that Isques, near that town, may be the site of *Portus Aepatiaci*. The absence of Boulogne from the *Notitia* is surprising, but the general consensus is that the *Notitia* lists from the mainland of Gaul are of later date than those from Britain. By 430 or so (the supposed date for the *Notitia* entries for this area) the importance of Boulogne's link with Britain had doubtless faded, and it no longer needed to figure in the list as a garrisoned fort. *Portus Aepatiaci* may therefore be identified with Oudenburg.

The last of the unidentified sites to which we must now return is *Grannona*. This, as already pointed out, must lie in the territory of the *Dux Tractus Armoricani*, and be the westernmost site of the *Litus Saxonicum* system. The boundary between the territory of the *Dux Belgicae Secundae* and that of the *Dux Tractus Armoricani* lies at the western edge of the province of *Gallia Belgica*, which must be at the border line between the tribal territories of the Ambiani (centred on Amiens) and the Rotomagenses (centred on Rouen), and it is probably to be found on a line which reached the coast near Dieppe. The area of land at the mouth of the Seine, and all the territory westwards of this, belonged, therefore, to the *Dux Tractus Armoricani*. *Grannona* is usually identified as some site near the Cherbourg peninsula, and recent scholars have now accepted the small fishing village of Port-en-Bessin, north of Bayeux, as its likely situation. But no trace of any Roman material has been found in or near Port-en-Bessin; and it is more probable that *Grannona* lies elsewhere.

If the identifications so far are correct, there were forts more or less equally spaced from Oudenburg (and possibly, if the Brittenburg is to be included, from north of the Rhine mouth) south-westwards along the coast of Gaul. All the major river estuaries have forts on them, and the flat ground to the north-east of the chalk cliffs at Cap Gris Nez is also well protected. If we include Boulogne as part of the original system, the estuaries of the Liane, the Canche and the Somme are all protected by a base for a fleet. The one missing estuary fort, corresponding with the site of Pevensey in Britain, is the one at the mouth of the Seine. For a strike fleet, the post at Rouen would have been much too deep inland; a fort would have been required at the mouth of the Seine to act as a Channel port, for both merchant and naval craft. At the Seine mouth lies Lillebonne, known to have been defended in late Roman times, though it was hardly a harbour site then, since it did not lie immediately on the river, possibly because the river had recently changed its course. Ammianus Marcellinus, in describing the Seine, says that it runs through Paris and then into the sea near *Castra Constantia*.[7] This fort has never been located, but the presence of another *Constantia* within 80 kilometres, at Coutances, is perhaps some indication that Ammianus has made a slip in his geography. Possibly in writing the geographical excursus in his history (in which this detail comes) Ammianus was using a map which showed *Constantia* as the nearest walled town to the Seine mouth. The Peutinger Table—the only copy of a Roman road-map known to us—shows this, and calls it *Cosentia*. There is then no need to postulate another late Roman defended site in this region which has left no trace.

Where, then, is *Grannona* to be found? It would be surprising if there were no fort at the mouth of the Seine, in the same area as the harbour now at Le Havre. Possibly it is no coincidence that one of the suburbs of that town has the name Graville, and there is a place marked on the Peutinger Table called *Gravinium* (if that is the right reading) which seems to be located in a similar area. It may be tentatively suggested that Le Havre lies on or near the site of *Grannona*, and that this is the Saxon Shore fort occupying the important position at the mouth of the Seine. Most of the known Saxon Shore forts are on estuaries, and as sites have been postulated at the other large estuaries in the northern part of Gaul, it would be curious indeed if the largest of them all, the Seine, was without one.

The extent of the Saxon Shore on the Continent, as shown by the evidence from the *Notitia*, is thus much the same as that in Britain. It runs along the coastline north-eastwards from the Seine mouth as far as the Rhine, and includes the four forts named in the *Notitia* as under its command, as well as the known sites of Boulogne and Oudenburg, if they are not identical with forts named in the *Notitia*. In its pages, the Saxon Shore is mentioned as a feature of the Continental side of the Channel, though the Count of the Saxon Shore had command only of the British forts; this would suggest that changes had taken place before the lists as we have them were written down, and that originally the command would have included both coasts. The possibility that the *Notitia* of the Gallic side gives later information than that for Britain may mean that more forts which once belonged to the Saxon Shore system have dropped out, and this helps to explain the apparent absence of such an important site as Boulogne.

6 THE DATE OF THE SYSTEM

To round off the description of both British and Continental defences, it is important to consider their dating. Certain obvious features—the thickness of the walls and the projecting bastions—align most of the sites described with forts on other frontiers of the later Roman empire. It is not possible, however, to point to exactly dated parallels in forts elsewhere, for forts of this period were not as stereotyped as they had been earlier: their plan was less regular and commonly adapted to the shape of the position they occupied rather than dictated by the buildings the fort contained. In addition, the type of defences which is to be seen in the forts of the Saxon Shore in Britain was in common use for more than a century. Forts of similar plan and layout might have been constructed at any date within the later Roman period.[1]

Part of the lack of standardization can be seen in the interior buildings. Whereas in earlier forts we have a clear picture of the standard layout and can account for most of the interior buildings, there is as yet only a very sketchy outline of the sort of buildings to be found inside a late Roman fort. The majority of buildings within the British Saxon Shore forts appear to have been of timber: at Richborough, Pevensey, Portchester and Burgh Castle there are more or less fragmentary traces of long, narrow, timber barrack-blocks, each of which had its own hearth. Stone buildings were few: at Richborough there was a central rectangular building, possibly the *principia* (headquarters building) of the later fort. At Lympne was found the only other stone building which has been claimed as a fort *principia*. It was not placed centrally, but in the northern part of the fort. Its plan was reminiscent of the shrine and official rooms which occupy the portion of a normal second-century *principia* building beyond the cross-hall and the tribunal (Fig. 54). The central room at Lympne has a polygonal apse, and this emphasis has helped strengthen its identification as the *aedes* (regimental chapel). This building, however, as it is closely paralleled by earlier *principia*, may not belong to the

Fig. 54 The so-called *principia* at Lympne. Scale 1 : 50.

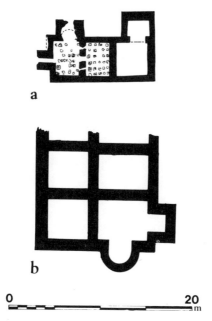

a

b

0   20
                                      m

Fig. 55 Bath buildings at Richborough (a) and Lympne (b). Scale 1:40.

late Roman phase of occupation of the site, but to a fort on the site connected with the earlier *Classis Britannica*.

Stone-built baths were commonly found inside the Saxon Shore forts. At Richborough, they were small and lay above the ruins of the houses in the north-east corner of the fort (Fig. 55). Baths are also known at Lympne and Dover. At the latter, a bath building was found many years ago under the church of St Mary's in the centre of the town. If, as seems likely, the line of the walls of the Saxon Shore fort at Dover was followed closely by the walls of the medieval town, this site would have lain just inside the corner of the late Roman fort. But another bath building, also lying within the late Roman fort, was recently found. It remains to be seen which, if either, of these baths was still in service for the late Roman fort.

The only other masonry buildings whose plans are known are at Richborough (Fig. 56). Here there are two buildings of the same shape but of different size. Each comprises a rectangular room with a verandah at one end. Excavation suggested that at least one of the two buildings had gone out of use by the later fourth century, and their alignment with the line of the road passing through the west gate perhaps shows that they are to be dated early in the period of the stone fort. The suggestion that the smaller and larger buildings are respectively a temple and a guild-room may be correct, but there is little evidence for either identification.

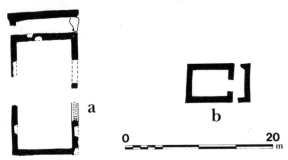

Fig. 56 Interior buildings from the fort at Richborough:
(a) the 'chalk house' in Site VII, (b) building in
Site IV. Scale 1 : 50.

One of the most important features of forts of the late third and fourth centuries was the water-supply; at many of the sites wells have been discovered and excavated. In addition to providing evidence for continuity of occupation finds from wells often form a very useful body of evidence for identifying the period of use of a fort, since anything dropped to the bottom of a well was probably lost by accident and was in daily use at the time of its loss. Water-supply was an important feature of the late Roman fort: to be able to hold out against assault or siege, it was important to have protected access to wells.

Not only in Britain, but also in the rest of the western Roman world, there is little information on any standard layout for the normal buildings within a late Roman fort. Typological considerations, therefore, both of interior buildings and of the style of fortification, are of little use for dating the British and Continental fortifications in relation to apparently similar sites on other Continental frontiers. However, there are abnormalities of design in some of the British forts which enable them to be given an early or late date within the group which they form. Coin-finds and general evidence from the pottery-finds from the Shore forts have led to the assumption that the majority of forts are assignable to the period 260–300. It is perhaps possible to be a little more precise.

Burgh Castle has been considered to have an early place among the group.[2] Its rounded corners and incomplete internal towers at the angle of the walls align it more properly with an early period of third-century defensive architecture than with the style of walls built in clearer response to the crisis period of 270–300. An earth rampart behind the walls in its earliest phase—if this indeed existed—is another indication of a relatively early date. But curtain wall and external towers alike are built in exactly the same style, and though the towers are clearly secondary to the main construction of the fort, they were a very early modification to the plan (Fig. 23, p. 39). Thus, though early in style, Burgh Castle was not built so early that it failed to incorporate some of the distinctive features of late third-century styles of fort construction.

Burgh Castle is situated very close to Caister-by-Yarmouth. This calls for some explanation, since if both sites were in contemporary use they are unusually close together. If, however, they are of different periods, it is difficult to see the advantage gained by siting a new harbour further inland, in a position in which a clear view of the sea was hardly possible. Perhaps the port of Caister had by this time begun to silt up and Burgh Castle was chosen as a suitable alternative harbour, tucked well behind the lee of the Lothingland heights. Alternatively, it may have been felt desirable to create a new, separate, military establishment as distinct from the civilian settlement (if that is what Caister now was) on the other side of the large estuary. In any case, it made tactical sense to have a walled base where troops could be billeted on the opposite side of a stretch of water from the fort, so that land communications and mobility might be relatively unimpaired by the large tracts of impassable marsh and river.

The style of the defences at Burgh Castle and at most of the other forts of the Saxon Shore is a wall-facing of blocks of stone with a square or rectangular face, or (in places where building stone was scarce) flint or septaria nodules set round a mortar core, interspersed with tile-courses; the latter helps bond the facing to the wall and act as convenient levelling courses during construction. This type of stonework, in small regular coursed blocks, keyed into the core of the wall by their irregular or pyramidal projections, but presenting a regular outer face—small blockwork—was not new to Britain, for in East Anglia, where building stone was scarce, construction of defences using split flints or septaria as a facing with tile bonding courses had been common since their introduction in the walls of Colchester. The style is well known,

Fig. 57 Line-drawing of the existing portion of the wall at
Bradwell, showing the stepping of the tile-courses at its base.

however, from public buildings of many Roman towns in Britain from an earlier date still.

Similar defences are found elsewhere in East Anglia, in the Shore forts of Bradwell (Fig. 57) and Walton (according to the sixteenth-century drawings which survive, Fig. 24, p. 41). Caistor-by-Norwich also had walls of the same type, and those of Caister-by-Yarmouth, though severely robbed, were probably similar. The walls of Caistor-by-Norwich, however, provide an interesting parallel with those of Burgh Castle. The details of their construction are nearly identical: flint-faced walls with triple tile-courses about 3·50 m thick at foundation level decrease in width towards the top, probably by a series of offsets, to 1·50 m wide, and an earth bank was piled behind the walls to facilitate access to the summit.[3]

At both sites the walls have external towers. At Burgh, they were clearly added to the fort walls while building was in progress, since they are keyed into the wall by a tongue of masonry at a height of about 3 m (Fig. 23, p. 39). At Caistor, the external towers of the town wall, alternately semicircular and rectangular, were thought to belong to the original phase of the wall by the excavator, and therefore to have formed part of it from the early or mid third century. But it is possible that they, too, like those at Burgh, are secondary to the main construction of the wall.[4] The similarity of Burgh and Caistor, while it does not prove that they were necessarily built contemporaneously, at least shows a strong family likeness, which may mean that both sets of walls were completed within not too long a space of time, and possibly even by the same builders. The external towers at the two sites may well therefore have been the result of a single defensive programme.

Various dates in the third century have been suggested for the construction of Burgh Castle but, even with a combination of large-scale excavation and exceptional good fortune with stratified finds, it is difficult to establish a closely dated *terminus post quem* for a fort's construction in the absence of a dated inscription. That Burgh belongs to a transitional stage of fort architecture is obvious enough from the diverse elements which it incorporates of both second-century and late third-century styles of fort design. Its finds, such as they are, suggest an initial occupation of the site not earlier than the third quarter of the third century. The towers, added on later, but by the same builders, suggest either a subsequent change in design or else an unfamiliarity with the planned external towers, perhaps never seen on a British site before. The corner towers, rendered useless for enfilading the walls by the curve of the corner, could never have been built thus if the builders had been aware of their purpose, and this helps to strengthen the impression that the site was built by local builders struggling with a fort-design which they did not fully understand. It has been suggested that the towers were added on after the construction of the fort walls in order that the heavier element, the walls, would have time to settle before the towers were put in place. But it was equally likely that the towers would sink; moreover, there exists an offset course of tiles running along the bottom of the wall, over which the towers are set, and which would surely have been cracked by any expected movement of the tower, once in position. The unfinished towers found at the interior corner of the walls and on the south wall show that a fort of an older style was first envisaged and that the plan was subsequently modified after parts of the walls had been built.

A similar modification of the original plan can be seen at Richborough, where one of the round corner towers was apparently a later addition to the rectangular corner. Although the fort was not built in the old style with rounded corners, the plan was still new enough to cause some perplexity when the builders reached the corner and were uncertain what style of tower to add. The arrangement of the tile-courses, as well as the evidence of an antiquarian drawing of this corner of the fort (Fig. 58), clearly show that this corner tower is secondary to the construction of the walls.

No evidence for such details has been found at Bradwell or Lympne, though the fort at Bradwell, with its rounded corners, appears to be of exactly the same type as that at Burgh Castle, and it could be that here too the towers are a later addition. The Saxon Shore fort at Dover, however, definitely falls within this transitional period of fort architecture. The fort wall here is narrower than those of all the other Saxon Shore forts, and the external towers are built in a completely different style from the walls, which had no tile-courses (as far as is at present known) whereas the towers had double tile-courses round them and are built of different stone; they are obviously a later

Fig. 58 Line-drawing of the south-west corner of the fort at
Richborough, showing the fort wall continuing behind
the round tower and not bonded to it.

addition. The presence of an earth rampart behind the walls, their narrow width and the addition of the external towers, show that this fort too can possibly be dated relatively early within this transitional stage.

If the provision of these forts along the eastern coast of Britain can be regarded as a comprehensive policy—a scheme for Channel defence—and not as a series of isolated phenomena built more or less at random over a period of thirty years between 270 and 300, then details such as the addition or absence of external towers in the first instance must be all the more significant chronologically, as must also the general style of building. The construction with *petit appareil* and tile-courses, as first used for town-wall building in Britain, spread from 270 onwards not only to the fort walls of the Saxon Shore, but also to the many city walls built in Gaul. Forts in Britain seem to have had no tile bonding courses until the late third century; it appears that Dover (to judge from its technique of construction apparently without tile-courses) is one of the earliest of those Saxon Shore forts provided towards the end of the third century. This is natural enough, since it is now clear that Dover had earlier been the headquarters of the *Classis Britannica* in Britain and, if it still had a suitable harbour, this would be among the first to receive the new defensive treatment.

This may be so, but there are also regional differences to take into consideration. The East Anglian forts are mostly built of split flints or septaria and tile-courses, partly because there was no other available building stone in the immediate neighbourhood. For this the walls of Caistor and Colchester provide sufficient illustration. Burgh Castle too was begun in the shape of an early third-century fort like Brancaster, though in the building style of a late third-century fort or town wall. It was further developed by the addition of external towers to make the fort, when completed, very similar to the series of late third-century defences in Gaul. The fact that tile-bonding courses are found here may be due to the shortage of other building materials except flint in the area and not to a conscious preference for that particular building style.

In Kent, however, there were other mid or late third-century fortifications besides those actually on the coast. There is evidence that Canterbury's walls were constructed in the period around 270. Previously this city had been protected by the forts at Reculver, Richborough and Dover: at Richborough there was a small earth fort round the triumphal monument which was converted into a look-out post, and at Dover the earlier *Classis Britannica* fort was finally abandoned and the new Saxon Shore fort built over it, closer to the river estuary and the harbour. At Canterbury, behind the city walls, was an earth bank in which was found a coin of Postumus, giving a *terminus post quem* of 268 for the construction of the defences: bank and wall were shown by excavation to have been contemporary. The wall was 2·10 m thick, built in coursed flints and mortar with interior towers, but without external bastions or tile-courses.[5] The similarity of this description to that of the walls of the new fort at Dover leads to the possibility that Canterbury and Dover were built at the same time. The Dover walls match those of Canterbury remarkably closely in both dimension and style and in the provision of an earth rampart which was no longer thought necessary when forts with thicker defensive walls, such as that at Richborough, began to be built.

The construction of the defences at Canterbury and Dover, therefore, as well as being a response to the same emergency, could also well be contemporary with the construction of the other related pair of defences in East Anglia. Despite the differences of style occasioned by the different building materials to hand, the approach to the defensive task seems similar: the first thought was to wall the site; then the external towers were added. But in all cases, the initial impulse was to use a style of defensive architecture which belonged to earlier days: in all cases except Canterbury, this was later adapted to the exigencies of a newer style.

By far the most significant parallel for the style of building of the British Saxon Shore forts is provided by the city walls of Gaul, particularly those of its northern and western parts. The features of British sites which are so distinctive—the *petit appareil*, the tile-courses, the thickness of the walls and the external towers are all found on many Gallic sites. One, Jublains, although an inland post, is closely comparable to the forts in size as well as detail (Fig. 59). It lay in a province which also included the Gallic coastal sites of Vannes and Nantes. Nantes has walls which have produced reused milestones of the early 270s from their foundation. The *terminus post quem* for the walls is thus 273 or 274. Vannes itself has produced no dating evidence, but another site in the region, probably built by the same builders and therefore contemporary, is more helpful. At Rennes, walled in exactly the same style as Nantes and others in the neighbourhood, a group of no less than thirteen milestones dating from the period 250–73 was found. This adds striking confirmation of the evidence from Nantes and suggests that this group of Gallic walls was probably built soon after 273.

The catastrophe which is generally assumed to have convinced the Gallic authorities that they needed to build walls round their cities was the growing series of barbarian invasions, and in particular the great invasion of 276. It is probable that the main series of the Gallic walls in northern and western Gaul date from the last quarter of the third century (275–300). Response to the invasion need not necessarily have been immediate in all quarters, but it is likely that the majority of the cities began to take measures for their own defence as soon as was practicable.[6]

On the whole, the Gallic walls are not as well preserved as those of the Saxon Shore forts: they surrounded the kernels of cities which have remained

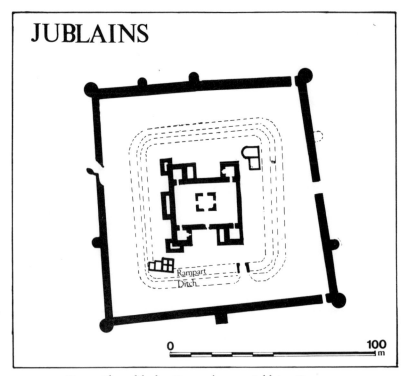

JUBLAINS

Fig. 59 Plan of the late Roman *burgus* at Jublains. Compare
this plan with that of the Brittenburg (Fig. 50, p. 87).
Scale 1 : 1800.

important centres from Roman times until now. A close examination of the
details of their construction is not always possible. They do not appear,
however, to provide as much evidence of a transitional stage of building as do
the British walls. None of the walls has a series of towers that can be shown to
have been later additions, like those at Burgh Castle.[7] The style throughout
Gaul, though differing from area to area according to the availability of local
types of stone, is yet remarkably uniform. In relation, therefore, to the walls
of the British Saxon Shore forts, the Gallic walls initially appear to be later,
since it might be supposed that, by the time that they were built, the style,
which we have seen to be unfamiliar to the builders of Burgh Castle and
Dover, had become so universally accepted as to become standard. The forts
of the Saxon Shore could easily therefore be seen as a transition between the
earlier tradition of fort building and the later style of town and city walls
found in such numbers on the Continent.

This is doubtless an over-simplification, for since Britain was an island on
the fringe of the Roman empire, new ideas in fortification introduced on the
Continent might easily not be fully understood or made effective in Britain

until a few years had elapsed. It is not possible, therefore, to say that the Saxon Shore forts are the 'missing link' between an earlier and later style of fort-building. In Britain itself this is true; but the style of Continental building need not have been affected by the style in Britain, even though such construction in both areas is of military origin.

The forts of the Saxon Shore in Britain are not only geographically close to the Gallic towns. They are close, too, in style, which the new northern British forts, constructed at the same period, are not. At Piercebridge, Elslack, and Newton Kyme, where new forts were built towards the end of the third century, an old style of fortification was retained: the forts are still of 'playing-card' shape, and though the layout of the interior buildings may have been changed to suit new needs and the width of the walls increased to obviate the need for an internal rampart, the defensive architecture remains virtually the same. The different style of the Saxon Shore forts is therefore all the more startling: there is something 'Continental' about them; they belong to a mainstream of Roman imperial defensive architecture, not a British backwater. The close connection with the Continent is hardly accidental: they are contemporary with the Gallic city walls.

There is one close link with the Continent of Europe at the end of the third century in the career of Carausius: as commander of the fleet in the Channel, he held portions of both Gaul and Britain. Some scholars have sought to explain this Continental connection by assuming that Carausius was in fact responsible for the construction of the forts in Britain. His were the new ideas in defence, his the experience which had seen similar defences rising on the Continent, and his the genius which transported the style to Britain, in response not to the threat of the Saxon and Frankish raiders, but to the threatened attack on his independence by the legitimate emperors, Maximian and Diocletian.[8] Barbarian pirates do not seem to be the type of enemy who would warrant such elaborate defensive measures being taken against them: the whole scheme of Channel fortification fits better with the protection of Britain from the recapturing forces of Rome than from the spasmodic attacks of pirate raiders.

Though this is perhaps an attractive theory, adding lustre to the idea that Carausius was the first 'monarch of an independent Britain', there are grave difficulties which, taken cumulatively, show it to be untenable. From the historical accounts, it is clear that Carausius controlled the Channel from 285, the year in which he received his command from Maximian, and there was no specific need for him to build his string of defences in the immediately ensuing period. Carausius' fleet ruled the Channel: the decisive battle would be fought at sea, between Carausius' well-tried fleet and the inexperienced new sailors of Maximian. To build a series of defended posts in Britain at this time was a counsel of despair: they would not stop Maximian securing a bridgehead on the island, and once that had been allowed, the struggle was as good as lost.

Carausius not only held the Channel fleet, but with it he had complete control of the approaches to Britain. There was nowhere on the Channel coastline where Maximian could build a fleet in 288–9, and so he had to build it on the Rhine and the Moselle. This fixed his line of approach along the Rhine, and although the system of defences in Britain was concentrated on the eastern coast, we need not suppose that Carausius' eastern-facing forts were designed to intercept Maximian alone. Only after the emperor had chosen the river on which to build his fleet could Carausius be certain from what direction the attack would come; in the short winter season of 288–9 there was insufficient time for building and completing a new series of forts facing the Rhine, from whose mouth Maximian was expected to launch his new campaign.

The presence of defended posts at Boulogne and Oudenburg (and perhaps at other places on the Continental coastline) has been taken to show that there was at the time a wider scheme of defence than that merely concerned with the Carausian defence of Britain. Carausius did hold territory in Gaul, and the provision of bases along the approach route from the Rhine—for Maximian and the Saxon pirates would come from the same direction—is only natural. Carausius' Gallic holdings were his most vulnerable spot and to provide defended posts on the Continental side of the Channel was for him a waste of effort, unless he could gain the safety of recognition as an equal by the legitimate emperors. If his propaganda attempts in 290–3 had been successful, he would have needed no defended bases against Maximian.

The British forts, if regarded as a strong cordon of heavily defended posts warding attackers off the shores of the island, are strangely inadequate. The Gallic city walls and many other town and fort sites in the western empire made skilful use of high ground when it was available: many abandoned hill-fort sites from prehistoric times were reused. When cities were enclosed with walls, they were usually reduced in size to include only those areas which were most immediately defensible. The Saxon Shore forts, however, are mostly on low ground: two of them (at Lympne and Dover) are positively overshadowed by high hills. Only Burgh Castle, Richborough and Walton Castle are on relatively higher ground, but even so are still very closely connected with the sea. We must deduce that the forts of the Saxon Shore, though garrisoned strong-points, were not primarily intended as defended frontier positions or refuges into which the local populace could flee to escape raiders; instead they were intended to protect harbours and offer defence from raids from the sea rather than from the attack of regular land-forces, which their siting makes them ill-suited to meet. If Carausius had intended constructing a set of impregnable defensive positions, he would have chosen sites which had better natural defences.

As the events of 293 at Boulogne showed, the vulnerability of such sites to Roman starvation tactics was decisive. Against a determined army, no fort wall was sufficient defence and, despite their massive style, these forts were not built to withstand siege. The coastal defences fit well into the pattern of late Roman military architecture over the whole of the Roman empire, and it is obvious that essentially similar forts found in other parts of the empire were not built against the Roman army. One cannot argue from the type of defensive architecture what sort of enemy the forts were designed to combat, but we can say that the barbarian raiders who in this area were infesting the seas (while in others they frequently crossed the land-frontiers) were very generally feared. Elsewhere, in response to their raiding, similar defences to those in Britain were constructed: there is no reason to suppose that the Saxon Shore forts in Britain were built as defence against any other enemy.

Perhaps the most telling argument (though this again is not entirely watertight) is that in 296 this system of defences was easily outflanked. If Carausius had built the forts to defend himself against Rome, they might have been expected to figure more prominently in the story of the recapture of Britain, and the fact that they do not is perhaps remarked on by the panegyricist when he poses the rhetorical question, 'Why did he desert his ports and his fleet?'[9] If Carausius had built the forts, the most likely time for him to have done so was in the period 285–90 and especially 288–9, when an attack was expected from the Rhine mouth. During that period there was probably no other direction from which Maximian could attack Britain. After the fall of Carausius' Continental holdings in 293, however, the way was open for Roman fleets to select a landing-place on the southern shore of Britain from any base they chose. It was then impossible to protect all the available landing sites with forts: the absence of forts along the Channel coast in Britain is particularly significant. At no time is there any evidence that forts were hastily constructed along the southern coast to adapt the defences to a more south-facing position.

The explanation, therefore, that the new series of forts was constructed by Carausius against the forces of Rome is unlikely. The forts could be of little use against the Roman fleet and are too widely spaced for effective precaution against Roman landings.

Nor is it really possible that the forts were built by Carausius against the pirates. The historical sources suggest that Carausius enjoyed some immediate success against these raiders, for as a consequence of his capture of them and their spoils a price was set on his head and his bid for independence made (see p. 24). This immediate success is hard to explain. Carausius received his command in 285, possibly late in the campaigning season, and his success was so immediate and spectacular as to cause his outlawry in the following year. This does not allow much time for 'preparing the fleet', still less for building

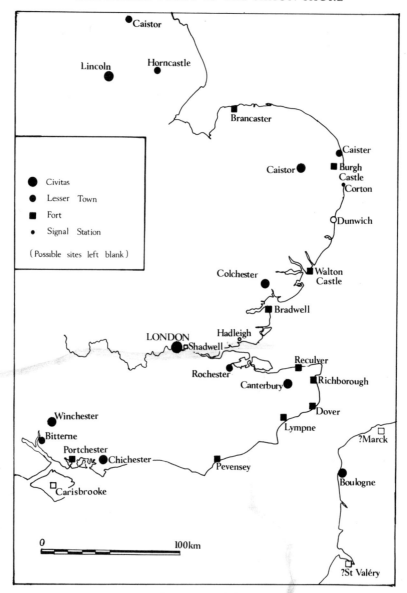

Fig. 60 Map of late Roman defences in Britain.

the series of forts before manning all the vessels and then scoring successes against the pirates. But evidently by 286, Carausius' counter-measures to the Saxon and Frankish raiding were working well. The space of a single winter (285–6) affords little time for the construction ready for use of the Shore forts against the pirates. The clear success which Carausius had in 286 will have rendered construction of new forts superfluous after that date.

The construction of the new forts in Britain and on the Continental Channel coast thus makes greatest sense as a continuation of the defensive policy started half a century earlier with the construction of Reculver and Brancaster (Fig. 60). In the later third century, we first have definite historical testimony that the Channel coasts were threatened by piracy: it is reasonable to suppose that the defences were rearranged to meet this threat. It is impossible to give an exact date when the forts were built, but the evidence from excavations at Richborough enables the date to be fixed within fairly precise limits.

In the mid third century, the site of the later stone fort at Richborough was occupied by a small fort, approximately one acre (0·4 ha) in size, surrounded by triple ditches and an earth rampart (Fig. 61). The monument, which stood

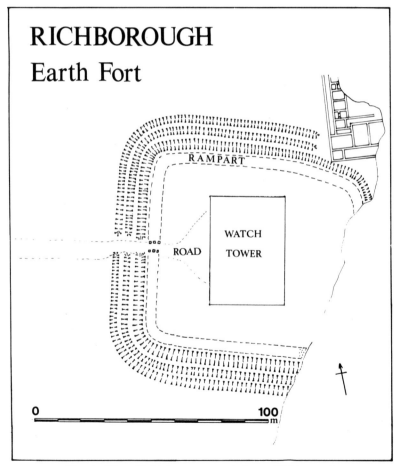

Fig. 61 The mid third-century earth-fort at Richborough.
Scale 1 : 1550.

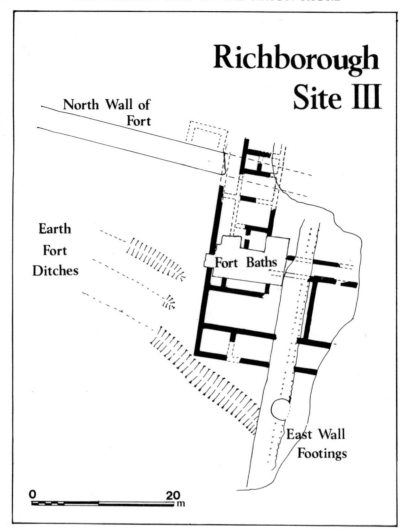

Fig. 62 Plan of Site III at Richborough, where the unused
east wall foundations overlie the remains of a second-
century house and the inner ditch of the earth fort.

centrally within this small enclosure, perhaps served as a watch-tower and
look-out post. Close outside the earthwork there stood at least one large house
still in use; the outer two ditches of the three are interrupted to avoid
damaging it. At some date in the later third century, all three ditches were
deliberately filled with the spoil from the rampart bank inside them as a
preliminary to the construction of the stone walls of the larger fort, which had
to be set on a level site. Evidence of the date of this filling of the ditches is thus
of great importance in determining the date of construction of the walls.

A detailed assessment of the dating evidence from the fill of these ditches shows that there is only a single coin of Carausius (found in dubious circumstances) out of over a hundred found in the ditches. All the others are pre-Carausian. At one point, the fill of one of the ditches was covered by the foundation of a wall, obviously intended to be the east wall of the stone fort. In fact, this was never used, and eventually the east wall was sited some metres further east. Neither in the wall foundation itself nor in a deep pit (probably intended as a well) cut through it was there any find which could be dated as late as the reign of Carausius (Fig. 62).

This most strongly suggests that Carausius was not the architect of Richborough, for his coinage, with its hopeful messages of immediate delivery from the troubles which were besetting the province, was surely in circulation from the very earliest years of his usurpation. The delay caused by the wrong layout of the east wall and by various other anomalies of construction was unthinkable inside such a tight time-scale as the brief period 285–6, and, if built later, the absence of Carausian coins from all stages of the work is inexplicable, considering the usual coin-loss at the site.[10]

If we admit that Carausius could not have built Richborough, and that the evidence points to its construction within the decade immediately before 285, then much of the basis of the 'Carausian' thesis of the construction of the Shore forts collapses. The lack of Carausian coins in what appear to be long-drawn-out constructional phases of Richborough, and their abundance in the earliest occupation levels inside the stone-fort, show that the walls were finished shortly before Carausius' assumption of the command in the Channel.

Such precision of dating within a decade is rarely obtainable merely from excavation. Here it is gained from the clear relationship of Richborough with the historical testimony about the period, and not least because from Richborough there are coin-finds in sufficient numbers to make the absence of Carausian coinage from the construction phases particularly noteworthy. At other forts, no such coincidence exists. The coin histograms, which show in broad outline the number of coins found per year of occupation (Fig. 63), point to occupation of most of the forts under Carausius. But this does not necessarily mean that he built them. The transitional style of Burgh Castle (already suggested to be an East Anglian version of a fort contemporary with Richborough) sets this fort equally early. Almost all the new forts, Burgh Castle, Bradwell, Walton Castle, Dover, Richborough and Lympne, were probably built during the decade 276–85, and presented to the new commander of the Channel fleet in 285 as the bases from which he could launch his offensive against the pirates.

The one fort in Britain for which a Carausian date can still be entertained is Portchester. Here, though coin finds are nothing like as abundant as at Richborough, there are indications that the earliest phases of the fort's use

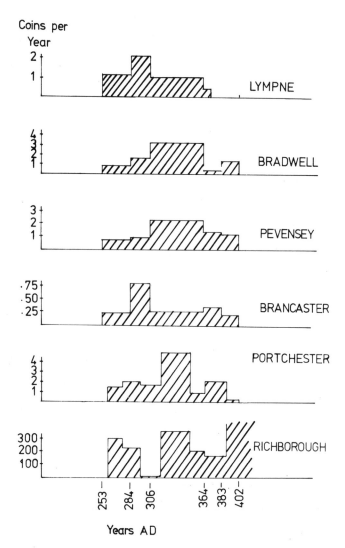

Fig. 63 Coin histograms of selected forts of the Saxon Shore.
(After B. W. Cunliffe, in *Richborough*, V, and
R. Reece, in *Britannia*, iii.)

were in the period 285–90, and that the construction layers, though containing only coins of the period immediately preceding Carausius, belonged to his reign. Layers inside the fort which levelled its interior ready for the construction of internal buildings contained Carausian coins.[11] But is this clear indication that Portchester was built by Carausius? It may be that Carausius had to complete construction and erection of the interior buildings.

The gap in the coin series from Portchester between 290 and 300 is hard to explain. Portchester, about 200 kilometres from any other coastal fort, was an isolated strong-point on the southern coast. Pevensey was not built to close the gap until the middle years of the fourth century (see p. 143). The position on the south coast would have admirably suited Portchester for a defensive role towards the end of Carausius' reign and during that of Allectus. Indeed, during the story of the recapture of Britain by Asclepiodotus and Constantius, the Roman fleet slipped past Allectus' ships stationed near the Isle of Wight.[12] The apparent gap in occupation from 290–6 shows that despite the presence of Allectus' fleet, Portchester was not used as its base. The failure to use Portchester in these years may have been a fatal error on the part of Carausius and Allectus, allowing the Roman fleet too easy a passage to the south coast of Britain in 296.

The construction date of forts on the Continental side of the Channel is even less precise. Boulogne had walls which were besieged in 293: their apparent connection with the harbour makes it likely that the part of the city which was under siege was the Haute Ville (see pp. 85–6). The topography of the tidal harbour at Boulogne fits well with this assumption, but although the Haute Ville was the only area known to have been walled in late Roman times, there are reports of other walls at Boulogne, linking the Haute Ville to the modern harbour. It cannot be certain that the *Gesoriagenses muri* of the panegyricist are really the walls of the citadel of *Gesoriacum*.[13]

Since the remains of *Grannona* and of *Marcae* have not been found, it is impossible to date the construction of either Gallic Saxon Shore fort. But in the *Notitia* list *Grannona* contains a *cohors*, and it may therefore be a contemporary of the only other fort in the Channel area which has the same sort of garrison, Reculver. Thus *Grannona* may have been built as early as the beginning of the third century. Brancaster is also an early fort, and it is perhaps significant that *Marcae* holds a garrison of *Equites Dalmatae*, like the British fort.

The first of the three distinguishable phases at Oudenburg has now been dated towards the middle of the third century. It was an earth-and-timber construction, possibly not rebuilt until the reign of Constantine, and not built in stone until the mid fourth century. Dating of the constructional phases of the fort is uncertain; the main evidence for occupation comes from the cemetery and relatively little excavation has taken place on the actual site of the fort. The phases of construction have at present been aligned with the major phase of use of the cemetery, which runs from the 340s until the beginning of the fifth century: originally the excavator wrote that the levelling layers of the second phase of the fort, before the stone fort was constructed, contained only pottery of the second and early part of the third centuries, together with a coin of Crispus (317–26).[14] Further excavation may show that the stone fort should be dated earlier than the present 'working hypothesis' puts it. One of the earlier earth-and-timber forts may have been the contemporary of the main series of British Shore forts built in 276–85.

When Carausius received his command in 285, with a brief to prepare a fleet, his facilities included command of a new series of defence works, probably lining both sides of the Channel, with which to fight the pirates. By now these latter constituted a very dangerous menace to the peace not only of the seas but also of the rich coastal areas of Britain and Gaul, especially in *Gallia Belgica* and *Armorica*. The post to which Carausius was elevated was a new one and although it is described in the sources as held 'along the shores of Belgica and Armorica' only, the defence of Britain must also have been included. The only way to suppress the pirate menace was by co-ordinated effort on both sides of the Channel.

In this light, the story of Carausius and his usurpation becomes the more comprehensible. If he received the bases as part of his initial command which was newly created, then the first use of the bases and so the first occupation on the sites would most naturally contain Carausian material, whereas the construction layers, as is the case, would not contain any Carausian material. The almost immediate success which Carausius won against the pirates followed his use of the bases to their best tactical advantage and his campaign, thus organized and using the new fleet, seems to have brought him ample rewards. Ultimately, the accusations of Maximian that he was misappropriating spoils captured from the pirates and the order of the newly appointed Augustus for his execution prompted him to trust his future to his bases and their fleet, and to rely on his ships to protect the island of Britain against the forces of Maximian and Rome. It was the existence of the forts round the coast of Britain which gave him the confidence needed to sustain an uprising against the power of Diocletian and his co-emperor.

The intensification of this scheme of Channel defence is, then, a pre-Carausian idea; its origins can be traced back into the early third century and before. Carausius' command, to be held at Boulogne, implies a return to older ideas on Channel defence, when the *Classis Britannica* was based on the Channel straits. The development of the system along the Channel coast in Britain and the Continent has already been traced (see p. 11), and the most likely date for the implementation of the fuller scheme is after the great barbarian invasions of the year 276, when Gaul was overrun and when the breakdown of Roman military strength may well have weakened the Channel fleet and so afforded opportunity for pirates to sail in and 'infest the seas'. Such a date would accord well with the correspondence between the Saxon Shore forts in Britain and the Gallic city walls and might suggest that both had their origins in imperial schemes for better defence of the Gallic and British provinces by strengthening frontiers and improving the defences inside the provinces. Thus the new series of defences might well have been ordered by Probus:[15] in addition to restoring the Gallic cities, he may be credited with taking measures to ensure the security of the coasts of Britain and Gaul as well. The prevention of further raiding was as important as the repair of damage already caused.

7 DEFENSIVE TACTICS

In previous chapters the Saxon Shore forts have been continually called a defensive system, and the presence of a series of very similarly designed forts round the coast supports the assumption that they served a uniform planned purpose. The defensive arrangements portrayed in the *Notitia* and described as the Saxon Shore are there quite clearly a *limes*—a Roman frontier system—since the *Notitia* itself lists the command of the *Comes Litoris Saxonici* under the heading of frontier areas. There can be little doubt that, whatever the origin of the name 'Saxon' in its title, this series of forts under the Count's command did at some period of late Roman history form a defensive system.

The presence of territory on the Gallic side of the Channel also called *Litus Saxonicum*, lying roughly opposite the area in Britain called by the same name, helps to strengthen the point that the Saxon Shore was a military arrangement. The use of the singular term *Litus* for these shores on both sides of the Channel is evidence of a plan which saw the Channel as one unit. If it was a local name which had grown up as a result of the Saxon settlements in the regions involved, one might expect the name to have been *Litora Saxonica*, for there are two distinct shores involved. Only some kind of military thinking would view the two shores as related areas under a single command.

If this series of forts of the Saxon Shore on both sides of the Channel was primarily built against pirate activity and above all against the Saxons, then the large scale of the defences and the new development of this type of military architecture call for some explanation. In this context, it is impossible not to look once again at parallel developments across the Channel. Though opinions have always varied as to the precise construction-date of the main series of Gallic city walls which are so closely similar to those of the Saxon Shore forts in Britain, there is general agreement that they were walled in response to the danger from tribes across the Rhine. This seems initially to have become acute in about 260, when a raid across the Rhine frontier by Alemanni caused a long series of devastations throughout Gaul and Spain, reaching as far as Tarragona, which was apparently destroyed at this time.[1] The threat was perhaps first answered by Postumus, who was then emperor of the separatist Gallic empire. He was probably responsible for constructing new forts of a temporary nature (he may even have fortified the monument at Richborough, turning the site into a small look-out post), if not some of the Gallic city walls themselves.[2]

The majority of the Gallic walls, however, were built as a result of the second great invasion which occurred in 276, when the destruction suffered by the hitherto unwalled cities was at its greatest. This left considerable debris and building rubble available for use in the new, and much contracted, wall circuits. Only one or two cities, notably Rome, seem to have had wall circuits before 276. Even these were provided under Aurelian, and not under Postumus or his Roman contemporaries.[3] In general, the evidence from reused material found in the walls of the Gallic cities supports the view that they were built after the invasion of 276. Many of the sites, for example Nantes and Rennes (p. 79), have produced finds from the foundations and cores of their walls which could not have been deposited before 273–4, at which date the Gallic empire no longer existed.

The designer of the British Saxon Shore forts was clearly unfamiliar with the style of defence which used external towers (Fig. 58, p. 101). Such towers were one of the main new features of the newly built forts. Towers at Dover, Burgh Castle and Richborough are secondary to the main construction phase. The variations in the plan of the towers (Fig. 64) show the lack of any standardized building procedure: at Burgh Castle, where the towers added to the corners fail to project sufficiently to enfilade the wall either side of them, there is evidence of a failure to grasp the purpose of the towers for tactical defence (see Fig. 22, p. 38, and p. 39).

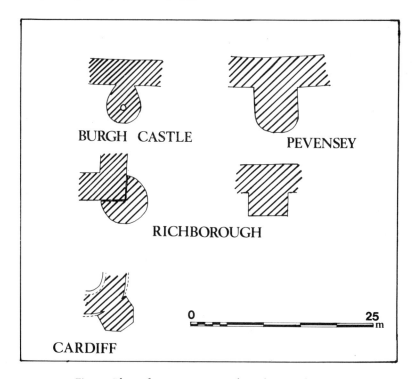

Fig. 64 Plans of towers in Saxon Shore forts. Scale 1 : 50.

The introduction of the towers was probably copied from their use in Gallic city walls of the period. To provide a secure chronological link between Gallic and British sites, more knowledge of the walls of Boulogne would be very useful. This site is crucial for the study of Channel defence at all periods. The main question concerning the later Roman period is in which defended circuit were Carausius' men trapped in 293? Was the circuit of late Roman walls on the Haute Ville built by then, or are there some earlier defences at Boulogne which have not been found and which belong to the time of the Carausian occupation? When we compare the archaeological remains and the plan of Boulogne (Fig. 48, p. 84) with the account of the capture of the city by Constantius in 293, it is evident that the story fits very well with the idea that the Haute Ville was occupied by supporters of Carausius at this time. Constantius constructed a mole across the tidal harbour-mouth to block off access from the sea to the defended area. This could quite simply be done by closing off the small inlet which ran north-west of the Haute Ville. This was a purely tidal harbour, since it was well away from the main stream of the River Liane which now runs through the city. Constantius' troops thus occupied the area between the Haute Ville and the present waterfront. Isolated from its harbour, the Haute Ville could not withstand a long siege. Topographical considerations therefore suggest that the walls of Boulogne were built on the Haute Ville before the siege of 293. The style of building, to judge from antiquarian reports, was similar to that of the Tour d'Odre (the Roman lighthouse lying north-west of the city) and that of the British Saxon Shore forts. The Haute Ville site at Boulogne therefore may be dated to the period 277–85.

The new style of the defences and in particular the provision of external towers imply the rather more widespread use of artillery as a permanent form of defence than had hitherto been the case. The necessity for such elaborate protection and fortification has sometimes been questioned; quotations from Ammianus Marcellinus[4] from the western empire, and Eusebius[5] and Dexippus[6] from the east, have been used to show the apparent ineptitude of the barbarian when confronted with Roman defence-works. Though these quotations from near-contemporary sources make a valid point, they also show that both Germans and Scythians were not averse to storming defended sites if it suited their purpose. There is some archaeological evidence from sites like Trier and Autun that it was not only the unwalled Gallic cities which suffered in the raiding.[7] Even twenty years after the main troubles, the city of Autun was still using British builders, made available again by the downfall of the empire of Carausius and Allectus, to rebuild public works in the city.[8] Even towns which had strong circuits of walls dating from the Augustan or later periods were not safe from the attacks of marauders and raiders.

The introduction of wall-artillery was in itself not a new thing in Britain, for its presence just after the turn of the third century in the region of Hadrian's Wall has been established. At Risingham, the remains of resilient platforms of stones and clay have been found, which can only have been intended for the emplacement of large *onagri*; at High Rochester, together with examples of stone shot, there are early and mid third-century inscriptions attesting the construction of gun-platforms (*ballistaria*). This shows that the use and practice of large artillery was well known to the Roman military command.[9] But the use of artillery with the new external towers was a refined art which had been brought to its peak of perfection many years before by the builders and defenders of Hellenistic fortifications.

Two main weapons were used by the Roman army in artillery warfare: the *ballista* and the *onager*. By the fourth century, the term *ballista* had come to mean the small 'cross-bow' type of arrow-shooting device, portrayed many times on Trajan's column and described in particular detail by the Greek writer Heron, whose name for it is the *cheiroballista* or 'hand-gun'. The weapon is mounted on a stand and set waist-high. The main part is, like a cross-bow, a straight channel or barrel in which the arrow runs, joined to a rectangular framework which houses a torsion bar on each side of the channel. Two pegs, set in mounts of twisted fibres so that they turn away from one another, carry between them the string which fires the arrow or bolt. The missile is placed at the end of the channel furthest from the pegs, and they are wound closer together against the spring of the fibres, so that the string can be placed behind the missile. When the pegs are released, they jerk apart, tensing the string and firing the arrow.

The *onager* is a far bigger machine, usually mounted on four wheels or on a cross-frame of solid timbers. It was a stone thrower with a torsion bar mounted low on the frame with a long arm and a container attached for launching missiles. The arm was wound down and secured, its container filled with stones and then released. The arc it described was stopped in mid-flight against a bar, releasing the missile. The machine earned its name of *onager* ('wild ass') because of the tremendous kick-back which it exerted. Another name for it, derived from its shape when ready to fire, was the 'scorpion'.

The torsion on both machines was provided by fibres, ropes, or—the best medium—twisted hair. The range of such machines appears to have been in general about 400 yards[10] and the type of machine which would have been most suitable in one of the external towers was the *ballista*, which could be operated by two men and had a wide range when set in the large type of open window found on most late Roman sites where towers with an upper storey have survived (Fig. 65 and Fig. 37, p. 58). A combination of these towers with *ballistae* could effectively control the environs of a fort and make any attempt at storming it very hazardous for the attackers. It seems unlikely that an *onager*

Fig. 65 Late Roman city walls at Le Mans, the Tour du Vivier.
The tower has been consolidated to show not only the large
U-shaped windows, but also elaborate patterned designs
in the wall-facing.

could have been mounted on a tower in the same way, since it required a far
greater amount of headroom for the swinging arm, and could not so easily be
moved. It also required a resilient platform such as would not necessarily be
provided by the wooden flooring of a tower.

The late third-century form of these fortifications does not approach the
complexity and sophistication which was later reached in fortifications in the
Roman world, particularly in the walls of Constantinople. The development
of fortifications in Byzantine times is well documented by several contemporary writers on the art of war. Rome's late third-century walls were useful
'for shutting out chance bodies of undesirables',[11] a description which tallies
well with the use to which the forts of the Saxon Shore were also to be put.

Artillery in the external towers of these forts not only ensured that undesirables were excluded, but, if properly used, was capable of holding them at arm's length. The towers of the Saxon Shore forts brought new security and protection to the bases and fleets of the men whose job it was to curtail piracy on the seas.

The artillery used in the towers at Richborough which had wooden floors was probably the *ballista*. Wooden floors are also presumed to have capped the towers at Portchester, while solid towers are known at Burgh Castle and Pevensey, and presumed to have existed at Lympne and Dover. The towers at Burgh Castle have large, enigmatic holes in their tops, and it has been suggested that these are the emplacements for large swivelling *onagri*, however machines of such a design might be constructed.[12] This, however,

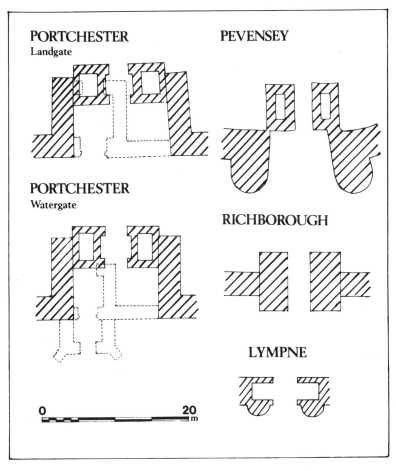

Fig. 66 Plans of gate-types in Saxon Shore forts. Scale 1 : 50.

seems unlikely, both because an *onager* needs a solid but resilient platform on which to operate (such as even a solid post could not offer) and also because it was important for the preservation of the fibres that the machine should be kept dry. There is little space on the top of the towers of Burgh Castle to take even an *onager*, and even less if there also had to be a roofed structure which still allowed space for the *onager* to swivel. The most that one could suppose might fit into the holes is some kind of *ballista*, but even that loses much of its effect through being fixed in a single arc. It is more likely that the central hole in the towers supported a timber superstructure and roof; such an arrangement would, of course, provide some handicap to the use of any machine, unless the wooden superstructure projected (like the medieval *hourdes*) beyond the stone-built part of the tower.

Comparison of the gate-towers of the forts (Fig. 66) affords an interesting study in the evolution of defensive strategy. The gate at Burgh Castle (Fig. 22, p. 38) consists of a single portal, possibly without guard-chambers, though more probably the reported 'retaining walls' found by nineteenth-century excavators formed part of the guard-rooms at the gate. If rectangular corner-towers once existed at the corners, then surely guard-chambers also existed at the gateways, as they must also have done at the earlier forts of rectangular

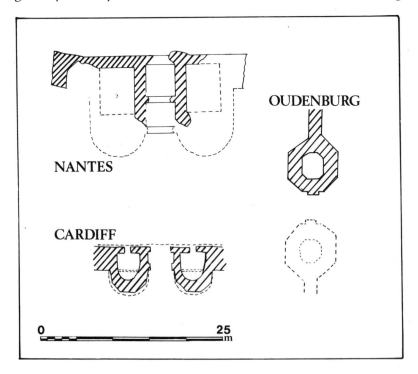

Fig. 67 Plans of gates in comparable late Roman forts. Scale 1 : 50.

shape with rounded corners at Brancaster and Reculver. Early drawings of the gate at Lympne, recorded at the time of its excavation, suggested that it could be interpreted as a simple passageway passing underneath a single large tower. Such a design for late Roman gateways is known from continental sites, in particular Zürich and the Wittnauer Horn, both in present-day Switzerland.[13] The recent excavations at Lympne, however (see pp. 54–5), show that this interpretation was erroneous. When one takes into account the considerable landslides which have occurred there, the reconstructed plan of the Lympne gate can be seen as a passageway flanked by a pair of U-shaped projecting towers which incorporated guard-chambers (see Fig. 66).

Richborough has gates with a pair of projecting towers, very similar in style to those of the late Rhineland forts of Alzey, Bad Kreuznach and Horbourg. This was the typical late Roman entrance—a single passageway deeply recessed between a pair of flanking bastions.[14] It is found in numerous examples throughout the Roman world, and though the towers which flank the entrance vary in shape from site to site, we can see further examples of the type at Nantes, Oudenburg and Cardiff (Fig. 67).

Nothing is known of the gates of Walton Castle or Bradwell, but Portchester has gates of a completely different type, unparalleled in the whole of military architecture of the later Roman empire except in Britain. At both the Landgate and the Watergate, the fort walls are inturned a short distance. The actual fort entrance runs between a pair of flanking guard-towers, recessed a little way inside the fort, but linked to the defences by the inturned wall. The design provides an open courtyard into which attackers had to force their way between three fields of fire to storm the gate. The uniqueness of design may not be difficult to explain. With the external towers spaced as they are, six to a side equally, a central gate defended by two further towers would make the aspect of the fort totally unbalanced. Architectural considerations alone demanded either a different spacing of the external towers to lighten the aspect of the gate, or some method of enfilading the entrance passages without adding extra towers.

The west gate at Pevensey can thus be seen as a logical combination of the last two types of gate. Not only does it have the pair of massive flanking towers standing guard over the entrance passage itself, but also a pair of smaller guard-towers recessed deep inside the enfiladed space (Fig. 68). If, as seems likely, the fort at Pevensey was a later addition to the defensive scheme, this combination of the best of both types of gateway is a natural one and shows that, even when the Saxon Shore forts were in use, defensive architecture was still adapting to new circumstances and attempting to improve on past designs.

Posterns are also numerous: most consist of a single passageway flanked by a tower, or with a tower in fairly close attendance. The postern gates at Portchester lie in the south and north walls and are of almost the same size as

Fig. 68 The west gate at Pevensey under excavation, showing
the guard towers. Note the lowest courses with the
criss-cross pattern of beams (now rotted to leave
vacant holes).

the main east and west enfiladed gates. They show that the elaborate care
taken to enfilade the gateways was not always necessary, and in the case of
Portchester may be as much decorative as functional. If the fort were ever
under attack, there would be no need to storm the cunningly designed main
gates, for the two sides were just as easy to attack. Similarly at Pevensey,
though the main west gate is an impressively designed structure, the east gate
is a simple arch which may not even have had interior guard-chambers
flanking it. There is no external tower to defend this gate as closely as its
counterpart on the west.

There are posterns at Pevensey and Richborough (Fig. 69), and at Brough-
on-Humber, which are defended by a twist in their passage through the wall:
this is commonly described as a *clavicula*—a key-shape in masonry. The
posterns in the north and south walls at Richborough are of similar type—an
opening in the wall defended by an L-shaped projection of masonry in front.
Similar gates are known from comparable gate-plans at other Continental
forts.[15]

The Saxon Shore forts, then, were heavily fortified guard-posts, equipped
with the artillery of the Roman army, and acting as strongholds for the fleet.
All the sites lie on comparatively low ground near a harbour, and thus they
represent defended ports rather than military positions sited to gain the
maximum advantage from an elevated defensive position. It is therefore
strange that the *Notitia Dignitatum* makes no mention of a *Praefectus Classis*
stationed at any of the forts. The exception is the *Praefectus Classis Sambricae*,

stationed at *Locus Quartensis sive Hornensis*, which, though not strictly a command belonging to the Saxon Shore, is yet so closely related that the fleet there mentioned must have had some duties in the Channel. Possibly the Channel fleet is nowhere mentioned because by the time the garrisons were listed in the *Notitia* the original postings had been superseded,[16] and though the fleet was originally based on one of the forts, it does not appear in the final version of the *Notitia*.

There is evidence, however, in the *Notitia* for a naval unit based at a Saxon Shore fort. At Paris, under the *Magister Peditum per Gallias*, we find the *Classis Anderetianorum*,[17] the Pevensey fleet, which had evidently taken its name from the fort at which it was once stationed on transfer. The existence of such a flotilla suggests that there was also at some time a *Classis Lemannensium, Dubrensium* and so on, each of which belonged to its own Shore fort; possibly these never moved anywhere. The Pevensey fleet was probably a small sea-going flotilla—perhaps a detachment of a larger unit which was spread out among all the Saxon Shore forts. If such fleets were small detachments only, taking their name from the fort to which they were seconded, it is not surprising that there is so little mention of them in the *Notitia*. Only one commander of troops at each fort is there given, and the fleets, though undoubtedly an important part of the defensive arrangements, may have been commanded by officers who did not rank high enough to be in overall command of the troops at any given fort. Only the Admiral of the fleet, the *Comes Litoris Saxonici*, in addition to the main officer in charge of a river-fleet on the Gallic side of the Channel, is named in the *Notitia*.

The choice of site for the individual forts is a further important point. Brancaster perhaps acted as a link between the defences on the Lincolnshire coast (which may in the later period at least have included the small towns of Caistor and Horncastle—though these were not strictly coastal sites—as well as a possible lost fort or town off Skegness)[18] and sites in East Anglia farther down the Saxon Shore. It provided a ferry terminus across the Wash, with a

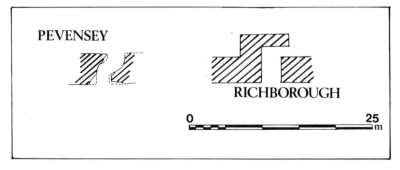

Fig. 69 Plans of postern gates at Richborough and Pevensey. Scale 1:50.

safe harbour on a very wind-swept coastline. Reculver, also an early fort, is a natural stopping-point even today for small craft, when easterly winds prevent the rounding of the Thanet headland. The Stonar bank at Richborough gave that site one of the most important harbours for cross-Channel traffic on the easiest route from Boulogne. Dover's topography has changed a good deal since the Roman period, but the Dour estuary was a good harbour until the medieval period, since when the formations of successive shingle banks have pushed later harbour installations out seawards. Pevensey and Lympne are both set on what must have been estuaries in Roman times, which would provide adequate shelter. Portchester was ideally situated as a harbour, shielded from the prevailing winds by the Isle of Wight, though it is reported that currents could make exit to the Solent difficult for small craft.[19]

A contrast has been drawn by D. A. White between the Saxon Shore forts and the Continental sites under the command of the *Dux Tractus Armoricani*.[20] He points out that from few of the British sites is there a clear view over the sea, whereas many of the French sites have exceptional views over a wide area. In fact this difference may not be fundamental: the Roman lookout from the tops of the walls or towers was some 8 or 9 metres higher than the earth-bound archaeologist of today. From such a height, most of the British sites will have had a clear view of the sea. At Burgh Castle, which is too near the Lothingland forest to have had a clear prospect, there was the neighbouring town of Caister to keep watch. Admittedly, there is nothing in Britain to compare with the exceptional siting of either Avranches or Coutances. But the apparent lack of any Roman harbour in the immediate vicinity of these sites does prompt a consideration of the relative purposes of both the British and the Continental sites. Among the places mentioned under the command of the *Dux Tractus Armoricani*, there seem to be three distinct types of site: first there are towns or cities which appear to lie too high on their hills to be closely associated with harbour installations, and which must have served if the need arose as refuges in time of danger. Second, there are bases like Rouen, Nantes and Blaye, which lie, like the British forts, on important river estuaries, but which are sited perhaps a little further upstream than their British counterparts. Third, only Brest, Vannes and Aleth occupy sites actually on the coast, although still on important rivers up which raiders might slip in search of plunder.

Most of these sites were not forts at all. They were *civitates*, or cities, in their own right.[21] It is hardly accidental that the forts unidentified from the Continental *Notitia* lists are those *in litore Saxonico*—the forts which were placed near the sea (to take the analogy from the British examples) in positions which were not necessarily ideal for tactical defence. Whereas the cities lasted into medieval times, usually as defensive positions, still bearing their old names, the forts dropped into oblivion, and may even have been swept away by the sea, as has happened to the British site at Walton Castle.

The difference in type between the forts of the Saxon Shore in Britain and the garrisons of the *Dux Tractus Armoricani* is remarkable, but it is not as significant as White tries to prove. He argues that there never was a comparable system of Roman forts along the northern coast of Gaul, and that the forts in Britain were unique because they were set up against the Roman forces attempting to recapture the island.[22] But any assumptions about the Gallic Saxon Shore forts are *argumentum e silentio*, and one cannot assume that because there is now no trace of the forts, they did not once exist. The two forts listed in the *Notitia*, *Marcae* and *Grannona*, together with the later additions at *Portus Aepatiaci* and *Locus Quartensis sive Hornensis*, may well have been elements in a system which stretched at its fullest extent from the Rhine mouth south-westwards along the Gallic coastline at least as far as the Seine, in many ways comparable to the British chain of forts (pp. 90–5). That the other garrisoned posts which figure in the *Notitia* lists are subsidiary to these Saxon Shore sites is clear, since all of them are towns, not forts, and were obviously pressed into coastal service as fleet bases and watchposts because of their advantageous position.

In addition to the fleets based on them, the Saxon Shore forts had land garrisons. It has always been assumed that originally these formed a mobile force, often of cavalry, which was to contest landings made by pirates if the fleet failed to intercept them.[23] In the *Notitia*, the only two forts recorded as having cavalry garrisons are those at Burgh Castle and Brancaster, where the unit named in the *Notitia* may not have been the original garrison.[24] Archaeological evidence for cavalry at other forts is meagre. The *Cohors I Baetasiorum* seems to have been stationed at Reculver for a long time, and presumably part of the *Legio II Augusta* was at Richborough from the late third century onwards, when the abandonment of the fortress at Caerleon was begun.[25] But the known garrisons of Dover and Lympne are thought to be the result of later transfers, and several of the other garrisons were possibly drafted in to replace a unit moved elsewhere.[26] It is perhaps significant that the garrison of *Marcae* on the Gallic side of the Channel was also of cavalry. Possibly the function of the mobile forces on either side of the Channel was to keep pace with the raiders once spotted and to be ready to contest any landing the pirates attempted to make. In this way, one or two strategically placed units of cavalry could deal with the threat of invasion.

The final link in the defensive chain is the signal-station. Without a series of these—perhaps doubling as look-out posts—the whole system would not be as efficient in operation. Many sites, particularly in East Anglia, have been suggested as possible positions for late third- and fourth-century signal-stations. Most of them lack positive evidence for their identification, but one, at Corton, had a ditch round it which contained late Roman pottery.[27] The site has now disappeared down the cliff. Some communication between forts, at least in East Anglia, was desirable if not tactically necessary; the Kentish group are near enough to one another to be able to send visual signals fairly easily.

A recent find at London confirms the existence of these watchtowers in the later period. At Shadwell, about a kilometre east of the eastern town wall of the City, the foundations of a tower 7 m square have been found. A watchtower on this site would have commanded a wide view over the Thames approaches to the City of London, and the finds associated with the building confirm its date in the last quarter of the third century.[28] This discovery reopens consideration of other sites of signal stations on the approaches to London. The site at Hadleigh, visible on aerial photographs as a small irregular ditched enclosure, may be such a one; but it could equally well be a small native farmstead enclosure.[29]

The tactical purpose of the Saxon Shore forts was threefold. They were strongholds and naval bases for the sailors of individual flotillas whose duty was to control pirate raids; they were garrisoned and defended bases where a body of mobile troops was ready to combat pirate landings; and they were an active discouragement, sited on the principal river estuaries, to penetration by pirates into the inland areas of both Gaul and Britain. Assuming that these forts were linked by signal-stations, a further purpose begins to reveal itself: the overall control of shipping which one might expect from a system which is described as a *limes* by the ancient sources. How, then, did the tactics of the scheme work?

The whole system as we know it is one which faces primarily towards the north-east—the direction from which the pirates, whether Saxons or Franks, normally came. The British forts are consistently spaced round the east coast, where Brancaster, Burgh Castle, Bradwell and Walton Castle would have been adequate to curtail the power of the Saxon raiders to penetrate up rivers in the area. Further south, the defences are more concentrated: the four posts of Reculver, Richborough, Dover and Lympne attest unusually concerted activity in the Channel and in the approaches to London at the mouth of the Thames. Similarly the forts on the Continental side of the Channel, at the Brittenburg (if it still existed), at Oudenburg and Boulogne, as well as at Calais-Marck (?*Marcae*) show that a parallel chain of forts was strung along the north-eastern coastline of *Gallia Belgica* between Boulogne and the Rhine mouth.

This, then, was the frontier: an extended set of strongly defended posts at key points along the shores of Britain and Gaul, which form a funnel-shaped defended re-entrant (Fig. 70), discouraging and ready to combat hostile landings in the coastal areas. As a system of defence, it has parallels with the

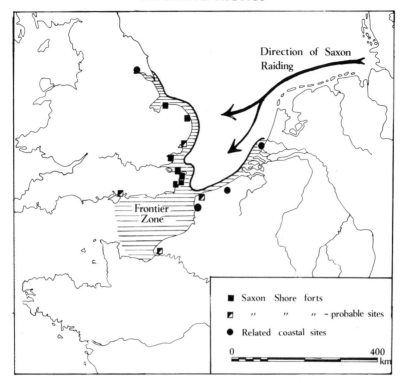

Direction of Saxon
Raiding

Frontier
Zone

■ Saxon Shore forts

▨   "   "   " - probable sites

● Related coastal sites

0   400
km

Fig. 70 Map to show the frontier of the Saxon Shore.

late Roman *limes* in the Julian Alps, where the main roads from Italy are
defended by continuous walled barriers which stretch from mountain top to
mountain top across the passes in a similar U-shape, with the central portion
and the roadway through the pass controlled by a fort.[30] The re-entrant nature
of the frontier of the Saxon Shore was possibly not as obvious to the Romans
as it is to us, since there was then no cartography accurate enough to provide
an overall view of such an extended system. It would have been clear,
however, to anyone sailing south-westwards from the Rhine mouth that the
coastline of Britain and Gaul narrowed at the Straits of Dover and then
widened again. That marauders following the coastline from the region of
Denmark would either naturally arrive direct at the Straits or else strike across
to attack East Anglia, seems obvious enough. The very topography of the
Channel invites penetration as far as the Straits, especially when a series of
defended posts prevented landing on either the East Anglian or the Gallic
coastlines.

The most important area for this system is thus the Straits of Dover. These
form a natural interception point, cutting off the access by sea to the richer
lands which lie in the southern part of Britain and the northern parts of Gaul.

Any pirate wishing to attack these areas had, if he was coming from beyond the Rhine, to pass through the Straits and to run the gamut of the formidable series of forts at Richborough, Dover, Lympne, Boulogne and *Marcae*. What is more, for a successful attack on a site on the southern coast of Britain, for example, the Saxons had to pass through the Straits twice: once in search of their plunder, and once laden with their spoils on the way home. They would have to escape the careful watch of a heavily guarded and equipped series of forts and look-out posts. When visibility was good, one could easily have seen from one side of the Straits to the other. When visibility was bad, the look-out system could not have worked, but the chances that an approaching band of Saxons would be spotted somewhere on their travels before arriving was great. In the time that it took for the Saxons to arrive, raid and reach home again, there could be many changes in the weather, and the journey must at all times have been a risky one.

The interpretation of the Channel straits as a *limes* zone explains several of the difficulties which have puzzled scholars concerned with the Saxon Shore. First, it has always been assumed that a series of forts at least as comprehensive as those along the east coast must also have existed along the south coast of Britain, and that therefore our information about the positioning of forts on the south coast is defective. It is suggested in a recent account that it makes tactical nonsense that Lympne and Portchester should be separated by about 150 km of coastline, filled only by the later fort at Pevensey, which still leaves about 100 km of coastline unprotected.[31] There is no need to assume, however, that coastal erosion has removed any forts in this region, since they were not necessary to the defensive scheme. Study of the *Notitia* should suffice to show that the defensive system was primarily concentrated along the east coast from Brancaster to Lympne, with only Pevensey and (if it is *Portus Adurni*) Portchester lying on the south coast of Britain. There are no other names in the *Notitia* list for which we have to supply British forts. A similar situation to that in Britain seems to apply in Gaul, where the stretch of coast called the *Litus Saxonicum* may not reach much farther west than the mouth of the Seine, roughly opposite Pevensey in Britain. The forts placed in the Channel area south-west of the line between Lympne and Boulogne were to some extent merely acting as a long-stop in case the *limes* system at the Dover Straits failed, for any reason, to intercept the raiders on their way through.

A second difficulty which is cleared up by this interpretation is the problem of the forts of the *Tractus Armoricanus*. These sites, unlike the forts of the Saxon Shore in Britain (and presumably also those of the Continental *Litus*), are not defences of the same type as the specifically military posts, but are city sites whose harbours have in most cases been pressed into service as fleet bases. The need for an extended series of defences down the north-western coastline of Gaul was not pressing while the Saxon Shore system with its *limes* across the

Straits of Dover was in full operation (see further, p. 149). The presence of forts of the Saxon Shore south-west of the Straits was necessary for the interception of pirates only if they were foolish enough to sail through. Once spotted, they would be chased and intercepted before they could land, or, if missed while sailing through the Straits first time, they would probably be captured on their way back, after the alarm had been raised and the forces on guard at the Straits were all the more on the alert.

There are echoes in the story of Carausius of the Saxon Shore system operating as here described, and particularly in the account of Eutropius:[32]

Although he [Carausius] caught many barbarians, he did not give their spoils back intact either to the provincials or to the imperial treasury, and when he began to be suspected of allowing the barbarians in so that he could intercept them sailing past with their spoils and thus become rich, under sentence of death from Maximian he assumed the imperial power and seized Britain.

Here is the system in action—the fleet is meant to intercept the barbarians at sea and prevent them landing. Maximian's accusations that Carausius was allowing the pirates to land and raid so that he could seize their booty must have some basis in fact. The system of defence based on the bottleneck of the Straits between Dover and Boulogne would afford both the scope for the working of the scheme and also the explanation of the accusation. If the barbarians landed and plundered, even though they had slipped through the Straits unnoticed, word would be brought back that there had been a raid. Not unnaturally the Carausian fleet would be on the watch for the pirates as they sailed back, laden with plunder, into the fleet's trap. The use of the word *admittere* for 'allowing the pirates in' shows that there was some area of guarded territory into which they were being admitted; there could hardly be a better explanation than that this was the area of the Channel, all but closed off to the Saxon pirates except by the thin stretch of water between Dover and Boulogne.

The accusation that Maximian made against Carausius therefore preserves some slight indication of the working of the Channel defence scheme. The charge against Carausius was a serious one; and if he were deliberately admitting the barbarians to this rich coastal area, it is difficult to see how he could have gained enough popularity to be accepted as the emperor of Britain. However, we have only the rumour, reported in a Roman and therefore a hostile source, that the admission of pirates was deliberate. Weather conditions could cause a breakdown of signalling or of early warning, so that opportunities frequently occurred for the pirates to break through the cordon formed by the Channel *limes*. After breaking through several times and learning that they had to run the gauntlet of the Roman forces on the way back, we may suppose that the pirates learnt the folly of slipping through the Channel block. When Carausius captured the barbarians laden with plunder, he was merely mopping up those groups of pirates who had dared to sail through the Straits under cover of conditions which prevented their interception. It is easy to see how malicious sources, wishing to blacken the name of Carausius (and attempt to turn the people of Britain against him into the bargain), might turn this to their advantage and accuse him of deliberately admitting the raiders. That he failed to return the money to the provincial treasury can be explained by the fact that coinage was in short supply and it may have been necessary to pay the wages of troops out of plunder so recaptured.

The existence of this system also helps to explain some of the details about the usurpation of Carausius which can now be seen as a natural consequence of the command of the Saxon Shore. It is obvious that Carausius enjoyed enormous and immediate success in his campaign against the pirates. There is evidence that the southern coasts of Britain and the northern coastline of Gaul were worst affected by the raids of the later third century, since it is here that there is a marked concentration of coin-hoards of this period (Fig. 2, p. 6). The perfect touch to this system of defence is that it was a static system: to control the pirates Carausius did not need to go on a punitive expedition, nor did he have to mount constant patrols over the whole of the Channel. All he had to do was to wait for the pirates to sail into the trap which was set for them. Of course this does not mean that the system was devoid of patrols. Its effectiveness would no doubt have been increased by the addition of regular fleet patrols in the North Sea, to be ready for pirates should they arrive. Indeed, Vegetius describes just such a patrol fleet when he talks of the ships used in Britain as scouting vessels, in which ropes, hulls, sails and even the sailors' uniforms were painted or dyed blue-green for camouflage, to keep their scouting activities as secret as possible.[33] It is easy to see how this system could establish quick and effective control over the raiders, who would soon learn of the danger in attempting to sail through the Straits and the virtual impossibility of making successful raids on the more exposed coasts of Britain and *Gallia Belgica*. They would discover that these were guarded not only by forts whose garrisons commanded the sea-lanes, but also by mobile troops to head off the invaders once they had landed. Carausius' success, therefore, was in great measure due to the effective working of this scheme, which was instituted for the first time when he was appointed commander of the Channel fleet in 285.

The pirates were a predictable enemy and this is what made the system of fortifications so effective. They had to approach from the direction of Denmark so that the siting of forts in positions to intercept their progress was possible. When Maximian attempted to mount his first attacks on Britain in 288–9 to oust the usurper Carausius, he prepared his fleet on the Rhine and

Moselle. To reach Britain, he had to sail down the Rhine and reached the North Sea at a point where the pirates were normally expected to appear. Ironically enough, he was sailing into the teeth of the newly constituted defensive system in Britain. It may equally well be this, as much as the bad weather suggested by the panegyrist,[34] which caused his setback and the failure of the whole expedition. Carausius' system of forts, while not intended as a base for an enemy of Rome, would have presented a formidable enough screen to the advancing Roman fleet; and Carausius' sailors, more practised in the art of naval warfare than many of those in Maximian's fleet, might well have found this relatively inexperienced force an easy prey.

Conversely, in 293, the situation was changed by the Roman capture of Boulogne. The line of approach of a Roman fleet now need not be directed at Britain through the Rhine mouth: with the loss of his Continental territory, Carausius lost also a vital element in the defence of Britain. He (and Allectus after him) was open to attack on his southern flank. By launching out from Rouen, along the Seine, Constantius could now avoid Allectus' defences and make surprise attacks which Allectus could not prevent, except by continual patrolling of the British coastline at all points opposite Gaul. In addition, with the confinement of Carausius and Allectus to the island of Britain, the trap for raiders will have broken down. In this situation, the absence of occupation between 290 and 296 at Portchester (p. 62), apparently the only Carausian base guarding the southern shores, is even more inexplicable.

As a method of controlling the pirate raids, the *limes* across the Channel Straits formed an enclosed defended zone of the peaceful and prosperous areas of southern Britain and northern Gaul. The pirates' mobility lay in their boats, which could most easily slip into rivers for surprise raids on inland sites. In East Anglia and *Gallia Belgica*, where there was no guarantee that warning could be given of the pirates' approach, the forts guarded the rivers and were ready with flotillas on patrol and mobile troops to contest actual raids should they occur. The main concentration of defence at the Channel Straits was waiting for the pirates to sail into the trap. Once spotted they could be chased and a subsidiary fleet at one of the back-up forts farther down the Channel sent out to head them off. Thus Rome's only maritime frontier was secured by a novel tactical scheme which took perfect advantage both of the area it was to control and of the enemy it was designed to obstruct.

8 BREAKDOWN OF THE COMMAND

Constantius' defeat of Allectus in 297 meant that there was now some reorganization to undertake. Reconstruction at some of the forts on Hadrian's Wall perhaps shows that some defences had been allowed to fall into a state of disrepair by Carausius and Allectus.[1] The coastal forts in the south, newly built, posed no such problems, and it is doubtful whether Constantius needed to concern himself much with these. It has been suggested that Constantius was the builder of one or more of the coastal forts,[2] but the presence of Carausian and earlier coinage as a prominent feature among the finds at the majority of the Saxon Shore sites suggests that the sites (and probably therefore the forts built on them) were in use during his reign.

From an organizational point of view, the appointment of further commanders of the Channel fleet must have been a difficult decision. Carausius' use of the fleet to blockade himself in Britain had been so effective that serious consideration was probably given to the question of how further safeguards could be introduced into the system to prevent future occurrences of the same sort. Closer watch must somehow be maintained on this powerful command, but it is difficult to believe that from now on the position occupied by Carausius was left empty (see pp. 24–6). In essence, it was no stronger than any exercised over any of the frontiers of the Roman world. The use which Carausius had made of his command was probably largely due to his personal claim on the soldiers and sailors whom he commanded: we are nowhere told how the civilian officials reacted to the usurpation, nor how other army commanders within Britain responded to his leadership. It is easy to over-estimate the reaction which Carausius might have produced in Constantius' and Maximian's minds. There is thus no need to believe that the division of the Channel into its British and Continental sections was an insurance against future usurpation. No doubt there were still commanders of the Channel fleet appointed until the consolidation of the post as that of the Count of the Saxon Shore.

At this period, other shores in Britain were also under attack. Large concentrations of coin-hoards of the later third century have been found in the west country and predominantly in the area of the Bristol Channel.[3] There is no historical record of Irish penetration into western Britain until the reign of Constantine, the son of Constantius.[4] According to Eusebius, it was he who pacified the people who lived along the western ocean—possibly a reference to events in Britain.

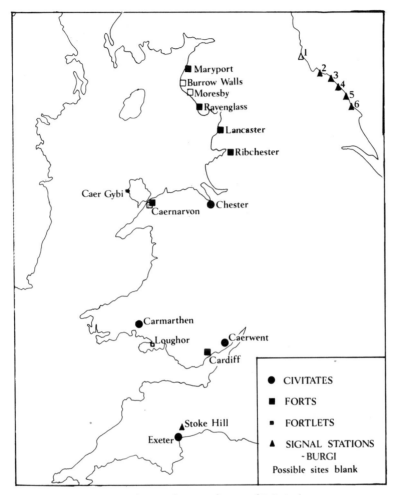

Fig. 71 New forts in the coastal areas of Britain (except
the Saxon Shore) in the fourth century. The numbered
sites (signal stations in the north-east) are
1, ?Sunderland; 2, Huntcliff; 3, Goldsborough; 4, Ravenscar;
5, Scarborough; 6, Filey.

The existence of forts along the western shoreline at several important sites
on river estuaries and coastal inlets is now known (Fig. 71). The fort most
closely akin to those of the Saxon Shore is that at Cardiff (Fig. 72), inside
which the medieval castle was built. It is roughly rectangular, though the
western side has a very oblique angle in it so as to make the correct description
of the fort a pentagon. The walls are 3 m thick and built of typical rubble
concrete work, faced with blocks of stone of medium size, with frequent

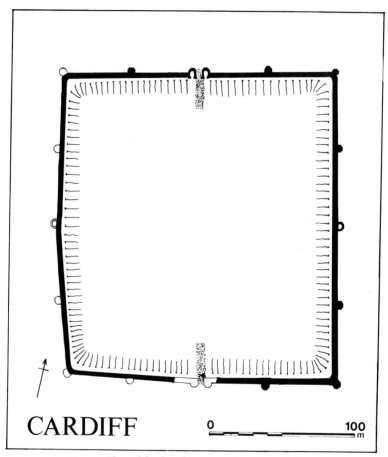

Fig. 72 Plan of the fourth-century fort at Cardiff.
Scale 1 : 2500.

lacing courses of flat granite at intervals. No tiles seem to have been used. The projecting towers are five-sided though some are founded on circular plinths: a study of the plinths and their relationship with the wall has shown that the foundations of the external towers may have been secondary to the main constructional phase. Above foundation level, they are bonded in. The wall-plinth describes an enclosure with rounded corners, and in the original phase there was also an earth-bank behind the walls, making the arrangements very reminiscent of earlier third-century forts. The gate-towers were also five-sided and between them lies a single portal, in which the excavators found evidence of several layers of road-metalling, evidence of a long period of occupation of the site.

At Lancaster on the River Lune, fragmentary remains of a fort of late Roman type have been found in a site which appears to have been occupied as a military base during the Roman occupation from the first century onwards. The late Roman fort was possibly rectangular with walls 3·5 m thick: at least one projecting tower has survived. The site has a good view over Morecambe Bay: its siting was ideal for both harbour and look-out post.

Other places off the west coast may have played a part as fleet-bases; Chester, whose defences are known to have been refurbished in the later third century, was a harbour-site as well as a legionary fortress and could have housed a fleet-base. Caernarvon, the Roman *Segontium*, had a fort of second-century date which appears still to have been occupied in the fourth. Within a very short distance of the fort lies another defended enclosure, apparently of Roman date. This site, until now unexcavated, may have been a late Roman stores compound, though little, apart from the style of architecture of the defensive walls, exist to support this conclusion.

In Anglesey at Holyhead, there is a fort very similar to the beachhead enclosure on the Rhine and Danube (whose exact date within the late Roman period is disputed).[5] Where they are found on the Continent, these sites are best interpreted as fortified landing bases: they are usually on the hostile bank of the two frontier rivers, affording a safe place for the Roman fleets or transport ships to cross. Caer Gybi, at Holyhead, like forts at Engers and Zullestein in Germany and Dunafalva in Hungary, has a pair of parallel walls running down towards the water, with a landward side, but no defence on the water's edge (Fig. 73). Despite its close affinity with these Continental sites, the situation on Anglesey seems in no way similar unless Anglesey were hostile territory on which the Romans needed to make a secure landing of troops and supplies. There is general agreement that such enclosures cannot date from earlier than Diocletian's reign, and most scholars would place them in the Constantinian period. Caer Gybi forms some part of the fourth-century

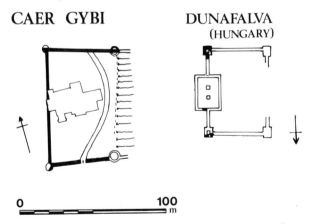

CAER GYBI

DUNAFALVA
(HUNGARY)

0 ———————— 100
m

Fig. 73 Plans of Caer Gybi and Dunafalva, Hungary, for comparison of the Welsh site with a known 'landing station' on the Continent. Scale 1:2500.

military history of the Roman west coast, but it is not possible yet to provide its context.

Further forts are known round the coast in the northern parts of Lancashire and Cumberland, but there is no direct evidence that they were used by the fleet to secure the western seas. The *Notitia* lists some of the forts in northern Britain, and it is clear that some of those which lay on the coast held garrisons in the fourth century, but of these, only one, *Arbeia* (South Shields), is recorded as having a garrison of sailors.[6]

In south Wales, the only new fort was at Cardiff, but other places also could have been used as naval bases. Caerwent, the *civitas* of the Silures, probably had a harbour somewhere near: Carmarthen, some distance up the River Towy, is now known to have been a Roman fortified town. Together with related sites in the neighbourhood, this too must have formed a more than adequate base for a fleet based in the Bristol Channel.[7] On the southern coast opposite Wales, occupation in the late Roman period is attested at Sea-Mills, though there is no fort-site known. At Lydney, a mosaic dedicated by Flavius Senilis, whose rank is recorded as *PR REL* (*Praefectus Reliquationis ?Classis*), attests further naval presence in the western part of Britain in 367, and possibly a stores base in the Bristol Channel.[8]

The evidence for naval activity in the western part of Britain in the later period is not great, and the mere presence of the defended sites does not of itself imply that Irish raiders were a continual nuisance from the late third century onwards. Nor does it imply that there was a system of defence in the same way that there was a system on the Saxon Shore to curb the Saxon pirates. There could never have been a system in the west comparable with that of the Saxon Shore, for the latter depended on a unique topographical situation. On the western coastline, which by comparison was indefensible, there was no obvious approach route to guard and it would have been a hopeless task to attempt to protect every estuary from attack by Irish raiders. The disposition of defence is much more comparable with the sites of the *Tractus Armoricanus* in Gaul, where it was impossible to stop every river mouth, but where existing forts, towns and cities were used as bases for a fleet which patrolled the seas, forever on the watch to intercept raiders. The exception is perhaps the fort at Cardiff, which does seem to be sited to provide a shore fort on the Bristol Channel, affording some protection to merchantmen in the area. It is commonly dated to the turn of the fourth century and may be an attempt to guard the sea-lane round the shores of Britain in general on the part of Constantius.

Throughout the fourth century there are scattered references to trouble from the west which had to be settled by one or other of the emperors, first Constans in 343,[9] then Constantius and Julian in 360,[10] Valentinian in 364[11] and again in 367.[12] As yet, no member of this defensive screen on the west coast has had systematic excavation, and it is not possible even to attempt to trace in detail the various stages and periods in which the forts and in particular the fort at Cardiff may have been manned in the fourth century. This severely limits the understanding we have of the way that the forts in the west were intended to combat raids in the area, if such was indeed their purpose.

The situation on the Channel coast in the later third and fourth centuries is difficult to assess for a variety of reasons. It is not easy to tell which of the forts were occupied at which periods without comprehensive excavation, but even then, one has to be exceptionally fortunate for enough of the upper levels of occupation to have survived to leave traces of timber buildings, which probably covered the major part of the interior of the forts (see p. 96). In addition, pottery finds of the fourth century cannot yet be dated as accurately as the Gaulish *sigallata* earlier in the Roman period, when enough is known of both workshops and individual potters to establish fairly precisely the date at which a particular piece was made. Fourth-century pottery in Britain is largely a product of local kilns, some of which were probably the centre of a wide distribution, but most of which sprang up as local attempts to fill the gap in the pottery market created by the collapse of the Gaulish *sigillata* manufacturers. For this reason, many of the fourth-century pottery forms are either imitations of the previous Gaulish types or products of such a functional nature that they are not distinctive enough to provide a chronological type-series. When distinctive types occur, they can only be dated by their association with coins and the few other closely datable finds.

Lists of coins found at a fort may seem at first sight a more promising indication of a site's history. But here, too, there are difficulties. The majority of Saxon Shore forts have only produced stray coin-finds. Interested antiquaries of the eighteenth and nineteenth centuries often had coin cabinets in which they collected coins from sites, and occasionally lists of these finds from Shore forts are recorded in antiquarian publications. In many cases, however, the coins themselves have disappeared and it is not now possible to check that the identifications are correct. When plotted as histograms (Fig. 63, p. 112), recording the numbers of coins found against the years to which they refer, most sites show two particular bursts of coinage activity, one during the reign of Carausius, who was the first to use the system, and one during the reign of Constantine. But the few coins found at the sites which have not been excavated may not be representative of the total number lost during the Roman period.[13] Only at Richborough, and, to a lesser extent, Portchester, is it possible to draw a histogram which records sufficient 'coin-loss' to make a significant contribution to our knowledge of the occupation-periods at these sites.

At Portchester, the relative frequency of the issues of the period from 300 to

345 and 365 to 383 suggests that the fort was in military occupation during these two phases. But this in itself spotlights the difficulty of knowing what a relative frequency of coin-finds during a particular period means. That troops were paid in coin during the Roman period is well enough established, so the presence of a greater or lesser amount of coins at different phases of the Roman period at the fort sites might reflect the presence or absence of a troop unit. If we assume that the number of coins lost in the Roman period reflects some roughly constant proportion of the coins which were in circulation at the time, and that the coins found by chance or excavation are an accurate picture of this 'coin-loss', then we can be confident in using these coinage statistics to show the presence or absence of troops. The coins found may be a random sample and enable statistical calculations to be made from them; but they may equally well (particularly in the case of the unexcavated sites) represent hoards of coins which had been collected in the Roman period, later disturbed and scattered by the plough, thus producing a distorted picture of the relative frequency of coins of some periods.

It is thus difficult to determine from the coin-finds alone whether there were troops in occupation. Nor is it easy to find clear evidence of military presence from the fort buildings. The barrack-blocks, if such they were, at Pevensey and Burgh Castle have not been closely examined; those at Richborough were virtually unrecognizable apart from a few irregular traces of mortar flooring, while the Roman levels at Portchester were disappointing in the almost total absence of Roman buildings of any sort. All that was found were slight foundation trenches of far from regularly planned timber buildings. It cannot be certain whether these belonged to an assumed military or civilian phase of the Portchester occupation.

Other independent evidence of the presence of late Roman troops at Saxon Shore forts is for the most part lacking. Examples of the late Roman military buckles, as found at Oudenburg (Fig. 3, p. 8), are rare finds at British coastal sites—the only published instances are from Richborough.[14] Weapons, too, are rarely found, but at several of the sites there are finds of triple-headed brooches, possibly connected in some way with military uniform (Fig. 74, from Richborough and Oudenburg). The frequent occurrence of these brooches in the cemetery of the fort at Oudenburg led the excavator to suggest a military connection: but brooches were necessary for men who wore tunics, and this style may merely have been fashionable, and not necessarily indicative everywhere they are found of military presence.

The best indication of the composition of any garrison in a fort is its cemetery, but most of the British Shore forts' cemeteries have not yet been located, only chance burials of the later Roman period.[15] The only cemetery in association with a coastal fort to have been excavated is the one at Oudenburg. This was an inhumation cemetery, containing at least 216 graves, the number which has been located and excavated. Of these, fifty were certainly male burials and twenty-one female, an identification made as much from the grave-goods as from the actual human remains (which did not in all cases survive). At least sixteen of the graves were of children under fifteen, and a great number of the identified males seem to have died in their twenties. The bodies seem to have been laid out in full ornament (note particularly the buckle and belt fittings, of which Fig. 3 is the most impressive example). But despite this presumably military characteristic and the presence of a surprising number of triple-headed brooches of cruciform type already compared with finds from Richborough, little else proclaims the cemetery to have been a military one. Weapons have been found in only three of the graves, and this absence of weaponry among men who were otherwise buried in full equipment is a surprising omission. It cannot necessarily be explained by assuming that the troop unit whose cemetery this was belonged to the 'regular' force of Roman troops, who would not necessarily possess their own weapons as would a more 'irregular' force of *laeti*—auxiliary troops of

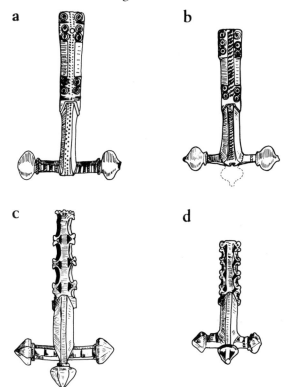

Fig. 74 Crossbow brooches from Oudenburg and Richborough:
(a) Oudenburg, Grave 27, (b) Richborough (IV, 65),
(c) Oudenburg, Grave 124, (d) Richborough (III, 19).
Scale 1:2.

Germanic origin drafted into the Roman army in their own traditional style of fighting unit.[16]

Coins found within the graves were mainly of the latter half of the fourth century and many of the other finds were of comparable date, suggesting that this cemetery at least was in use from 340 to 410. Another cemetery, as yet not fully explored, lies nearby, and, to judge from the few discoveries so far, is earlier in date. Despite the lack of definite evidence that this cemetery was that of a troop unit, the presence of a coin-hoard which held a considerable percentage of issues from eastern mints gave some slight indication that some of the men buried there had been stationed in an easterly area in the 370s and 380s. One of the units which had served with Valentinian in the east was the *milites Nerviorum*, who are found in the *Notitia* to be stationed at *Portus Aepatiaci*, in the command of the *Dux Belgicae Secundae*. This coin-hoard with its eastern coins (relatively uncommon in the western empire) thus provides some albeit circumstantial evidence that Oudenburg was the *Notitia* fort of *Portus Aepatiaci*, and that its garrison and some of the men buried in the cemetery were *milites Nerviorum*.

Consideration of the contents of this cemetery also raises the question of how one determines during which periods the forts were in use, even supposing that it can be taken as certain that there were troops there at any period. At Portchester, periods of 'tidy' occupation alternated with intervals when domestic rubbish was allowed to pile up inside the fort. The cleaner phase of occupation suggests a time when troops were in occupation of the site. This, taken with the coin evidence, leads to the conclusion that the early years of the fourth century, from 300 to 345, were the period of maximum military activity there.

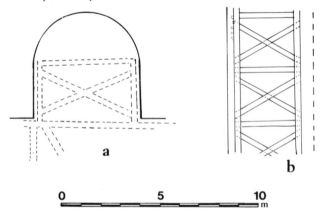

Fig. 75 Plan of wooden beams used in the foundation
courses at Pevensey: (a) under the towers,
(b) under the walls.

The evidence from Pevensey, Portchester's neighbour on the south coast, gives a completely different picture. We have already seen that the fort was one of the named sites in the list of the *Comes Litoris Saxonici* in the *Notitia* (p. 66) and that it was originally the base for a fleet which retained its name even though later moved to a new position (p. 70). Archaeological evidence—a coin found under the walls in one of the holes formed by the timber beams (Fig. 75)—suggests that the fort was added later than all the other sites which lay in the Saxon Shore system on the south coast of Britain. The coin, an issue of Constantine's later years as emperor, gives a date after which the fort must have been constructed. Pevensey, on this evidence, was built no earlier than 335. Probably the decision to add another fort closer to the Channel Straits than Portchester was aimed at providing a further back-up post for the defensive system.

It cannot be certain, however, that the evidence of this single coin is trustworthy. The initial occupation layers on the site at Pevensey have produced surprising numbers of coins of Carausius for a site which is supposed to have been built some forty years after the death of the usurper, and it would have been relatively easy for a small object like a coin to have rolled or have been pushed (possibly by animal action) into a cavity formed by the decay of one of the timber baulks in the wall foundation. Nonetheless, Pevensey is a fort which shows some of the most advanced defensive architecture on the Saxon Shore: its walls are now (and probably originally were) higher than those of others of the series, and the gate is a highly developed form of the same type as is found at Portchester (Fig. 66, p. 121), thus establishing its late place in the series. Whether it was really built as many as forty years later than the rest of the forts only further, more comprehensive excavation will tell.

The way in which other sites on the south coast fit into the defensive picture is also unclear. An enclosure of what seems to be typical Roman shape lies under the Norman mound of Carisbrooke Castle (Fig. 76). This, too, has been claimed to have played some part in the Roman coastal system of defence, whether in the fourth century or earlier.[17] Despite the 'Roman' features—its 'playing-card' shape, its inturned entrances and the slight traces of externally projecting towers—there is little indication that the enclosure is of Roman date. Despite excavation, admittedly limited by the presence of the Norman mound which virtually conceals it, there is very little trace of Roman pottery from the site: a wealth of pottery is a keynote of most of the Saxon Shore sites and it is this lack which calls the Roman origin of Carisbrooke most clearly into question. The site is not near the coast; it lies in the centre of the Isle of Wight and, if a Roman site and not a small early Saxon 'burgh', is perhaps better seen as a watch-tower or a refuge for the local population of the island in Roman times, rather than a fort.

Another site defended in the Roman period lies at Bitterne, on a bend of the

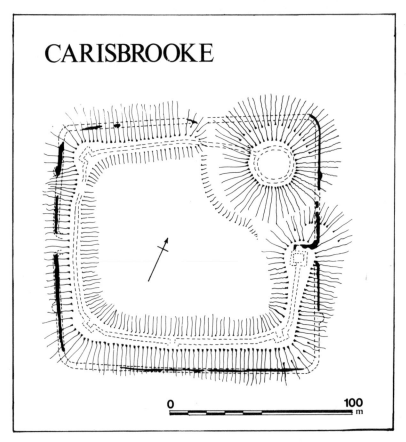

CARISBROOKE

Fig. 76 Plan of the 'fort' at Carisbrooke. Scale 1:2000.

River Itchen, close to the point where it joins Southampton Water. The walled site (Fig. 77) occupies a triangular area in the bend of the river. Its walls are massive, built in a style similar to that of Pevensey; from the construction levels, coins of the emperor Valens have been found, an indication that the fort must have been built after 365. Little excavation has been possible at this site on the area inside the defences, with the result that little can be said about its possible use and the part which it may have played in the Channel defensive scheme.

The commander of this frontier system is likely to have been a *Dux* in control of *limitanei*, 'frontier troops'. Carausius was presumably the prototype for the creation of this command, but the post cannot have been so different from that of the commander of the *Classis Britannica* of earlier days. In the *Notitia*, the commander is given the title of *Comes*, a higher rank than that of *Dux*: the difference was that whereas the *Dux* was normally in command only of the static frontier troops, the *Comes* would have *comitatenses*—units of the field army—under his command as well. Thus, though remaining basically a frontier command, the Saxon Shore was elevated during the course of the fourth century by the appointment of a *Comes* rather than a *Dux*.

We have already seen also that there are two forts of the 'Saxon Shore' system which lie on the Gallic side of the Channel, and it is reasonable to suppose that they once formed part of the command of the *Dux* or the *Comes*: if they did not come by their name from their original inclusion in the fuller system, it is difficult adequately to explain their additional title. In the *Notitia*, these two forts lie in the territory and under the command of the two Continental commanders, the *Dux Tractus Armoricani* and the *Dux Belgicae Secundae*. They must have been transferred and the Saxon Shore command broken up by the time that the *Notitia* was written—probably by about 395.

There were therefore two changes in the defensive strategy in the fourth century. It is more than likely that the commander of the Saxon Shore was elevated from a *Dux* to a *Comes* at some time when he still held control of the Gallic side of the Channel. As the commander of a large stretch of very unmanageable frontier, he would need special powers and the mobility of

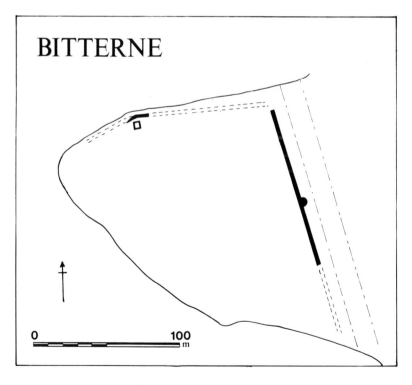

Fig. 77 Plan of the late Roman site at Bitterne. Scale 1 : 2500.

troops afforded by the change of rank to allow him to command *comitatenses* as a general rule. The office of *Comes* was a development forwarded by Constantine, and it was under that emperor or his sons that the promotion was probably instituted. Constans visited Britain in a hurry in the winter of 342–3;[18] it may have been the imperial visit which sparked off new and tighter defensive measures on the Channel coast with the construction of Pevensey and the consolidation of the Saxon Shore command by the elevation of its commander to Comitival status.

Historical sources show that the Saxon Shore was one of the main areas still open to barbarian attack during the fourth century. Ammianus Marcellinus, writing towards the end of the same century, records the 'barbarian conspiracy' of 367, in which Picts, Attecotti and Scotti attacking from the north and west were joined by Franks (and presumably Saxons) who attacked the south-east.[19] It is not exactly clear which areas of Britain were under attack from the Franks, for Ammianus' phrase describing this region—'the Gallic areas'—is ambiguous. But wherever the attack, whether on Gaul or on Britain, it must have affected territory under the control of the *Comes Litoris Saxonici*, for at this date he probably still held the Gallic as well as the British shores. The attack was successful: the barbarians took a *Dux* prisoner, and killed Nectaridus, described by Ammianus as the 'count of the maritime areas'. This seems to be an obvious alternative for 'Count of the Saxon Shore', to explain the term better for a wider audience. It took a year of hard campaigning to set the situation in Britain to rights and by the end of 368[20] Count Theodosius had restored an uneasy peace, though at the expense of withdrawing troops from some of the more outlying forts beyond Hadrian's Wall. Such withdrawals became more and more commonplace as the fourth century wore on: gradually the army of Britain was whittled away and not replaced, for a variety of reasons, military, strategic or even as a result of unsuccessful claims to imperial power by men who took troops from Britain to fight for their cause. In 383, this happened when Magnus Maximus fought for the primacy over Gratian and lost. Further raids from Picts and Scots in the period after Maximus' death prompted appeals from Britain for help. Possibly as a result of this, in 396–8, the Roman general Stilicho, in charge of the emperor's troops, made a successful expedition against the Irish and the Saxons.[21] But such military action, though short, sharp and thorough, cannot have had a lasting effect. The Romans were again expelled from Britain—an event which possibly led to the famous letter from the emperor Honorius to Britain in 410, telling the *civitates* to look to their own defence and to expect no further help from Rome.[22]

The presence of tiles from Pevensey stamped *HON AUG ANDRIA* (Fig. 78), of which one complete example exists and shattered pieces were found during excavation in 1906–8, have been generally thought to read *Hon[orius]*

Fig. 78 Tile-stamps reading *HON AUG ANDRIA*, from
Pevensey. Scale 1:2.

Aug[ustus] And[e]ri[d]a, attesting reconstruction at the site late in the fourth
century. But the tiles are now suspect, since tests on them have shown that
they are probably modern forgeries: a thermoluminescent dating test has
given results which show that the tiles were made about 70 years ago.[23] The
complete example was supposedly found by chance by Charles Dawson, who
was implicated in the Piltdown forgery, and the shattered fragments, though
found in excavation by a reputable scholar, may have been planted for him to
find. The evidence which has for so long been thought to substantiate some
rebuilding of the fort at Pevensey under Honorius is no longer valid: there is
little to suggest that any of the forts were substantially rebuilt or adapted to
the different situation in the later fourth century.

The name *Litus Saxonicum* occurs only in the *Notitia*, a document which
appears from its format to have been intended for official use by both military
and civilian dignitaries. It is perhaps curious that Ammianus, describing the
events of 367, almost goes out of his way not to mention the official title of the
Comes who was killed in the raids: could it be that the name for the defensive
system was not yet in use?

That the name has some pedigree is certain from the *Notitia*, for the forts on
the Gallic coastline 'on the Saxon Shore' would not preserve this title unless it
had some honorific purpose. It has been claimed that the two forts, *Grannona*
and *Marcae*, were described as being 'on the Saxon Shore' because of the
Saxon settlement which is known to have occurred precisely in the Bessin and
the Boulonnais, areas in which the respective forts must have lain, though
their exact sites are in doubt. But the fact that the *Litus Saxonicum* in the *Notitia*
manifestly refers to a frontier system suggests that forts so named will have
been integrated within that system even though later transferred to another
command. In any case, there is nothing incompatible with the view that the
Litus Saxonicum refers to a shore under Saxon attack and that which seeks to
explain it as 'the shore settled by Saxons'. Both may, and probably did, occur,
and to a limited extent the two roles may have been contemporary. There is at
present little evidence of Saxon settlement during the fourth century in
Britain, and none at all in Gaul. The series of forts of the Saxon Shore, the
majority of which are known to have been built in the later third century, are
unlikely to have been originally planned as posts to 'watch over' Saxon
settlement, whatever such control is supposed to have meant. In other areas of

the Roman world, the presence of imported barbarian tribes as settlers is marked by the absence of regular Roman fortifications to keep guard over 'unruly' settlers.

It is thus improbable that the name 'Saxon Shore' grew up originally because of the number of Saxons who were settling on the eastern and southern coasts of Britain. By 395, the date of the name's use in the *Notitia*, it was sufficiently current to have stuck to the pair of Gallic forts despite their transfer to other commanders. The name is admittedly unusual in that it is the

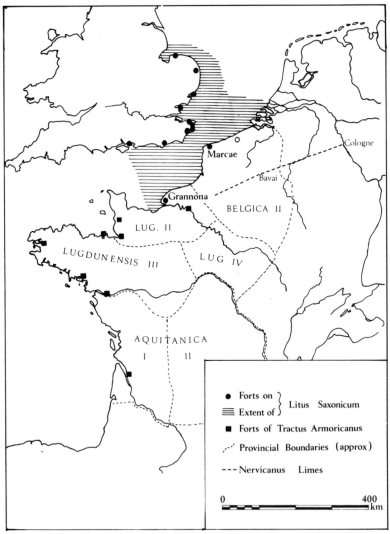

Fig. 79 The commands of the *Comes Litoris Saxonici* and the *Dux Tractus Armoricani*, possibly in existence contemporaneously.

only clear example of a late Roman frontier which is given the name of its attackers: perhaps this name became current first of all through local usage, and only later became crystallized into official military parlance. The reason why Ammianus did not use the name may be as much the fact that the command was beginning to break up at the time when he wrote: with the lack of control over Britain towards the end of the fourth century, it is easy to see that the system of cutting the raiders off at the Straits of Dover would break down.

The question of the date at which the Saxon Shore command broke up into its British and Continental parts is equally difficult to answer. We do not know the date at which the two Continental *Duces* were first appointed: slight indication that it was an older command is evident from the full title of the *Dux Tractus Armoricani et Nervicani limitis*. The *Nervicanus limes*, presumably the line of fortified posts along the road from Cologne to Bavai (which was originally the *Civitas Nerviorum*, though in the later Roman period it shrank and became merely a fort), is properly within the territory of the *Dux Belgicae Secundae*.

Comparison has rightly in the past been drawn between the forts of the Saxon Shore in Britain and the posts of the *Tractus Armoricanus* in Gaul. The British sites seem to be purpose-built forts whereas the posts of the Gallic Shore are merely *civitates* or towns and ports adapted for use as troop and fleet bases.[24] The difference is striking and it is the same sort of difference between the Saxon Shore forts and the series of bases along the western coast of Britain, where defence was not so easily planned. In consideration of the Continental defences, it is important to remember that the Romans lost control of Britain before the collapse of their power in Gaul. Defence against the Saxon continued in Gaul well into the fifth century along parts, if not all, of the *Tractus Armoricanus*: thus, though the bottleneck at the Channel Straits had broken down, the importance of coastal defence was increased in the later period. The immediate mobilization of many of the available harbours and coastal sites to meet the emergency was the only solution: thus the posts of the *Dux Tractus Armoricani* came into their own.

It is possible that the commands of the *Comes* (or *Dux*) *Litoris Saxonici* and the *Dux Tractus Armoricani* are complementary (Fig. 79). If the *Comes* held the clearly defined frontier areas actually on the coast, at the Channel Straits and the immediate back-up forts inside the protected zone of the Channel, then the *Dux* can be seen to hold an area which lies immediately to the rear of this, particularly if we take into account the possibility that he also held the *Nervicanus limes*. The loose string of Gallic defences down the coast would have been adequate for the eventual mopping up of any Saxons who strayed through the Straits and did not immediately return. Later (Fig. 80), this situation was dramatically changed: a new command, that of the *Dux Belgicae Secundae*, was created to take over the area originally controlled by the Count

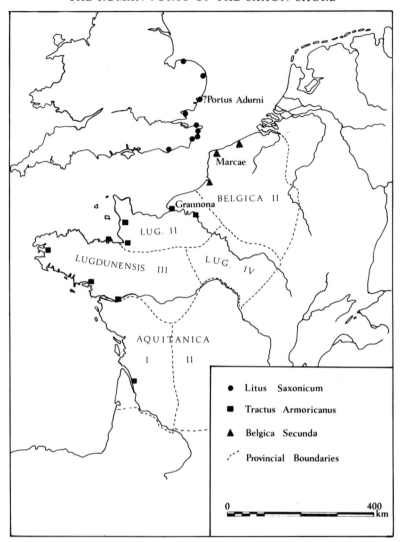

Fig. 80 The full series of command in the coastal area
according to the *Notitia*.

of the Saxon Shore, whose activities were now confined solely to Britain.[25]
This area must have been exceptionally difficult to control to warrant such
special treatment; it was the preserve of *laeti*—Germanic settlers who were
bound to produce troops on a mercenary basis for Rome's auxiliary armies.[26]
The *civitates* of the area were tucked for the most part well inland. Some, like
the *Nervii* and the *Menapii*, seem to have been virtually eclipsed by the needs of
the frontier. With the loss of Britain, this area will have become harder and
harder to keep under effective control.[27]

The provision of a small defended post on Alderney in the Channel Islands might well fit into this defensive scheme at this late date. If it really is a Roman site, the fort at the Nunnery on Alderney (Fig. 47, p. 82) could be an attempt to provide advance warning of the pirates' approach to the towns on the western shores of Brittany and the western side of the Cherbourg peninsula. In form, the site is remarkably similar to the outer enclosures of a set of signal stations found on the east coast of Britain in Yorkshire and Humberside (Fig. 81). Excavations at two of them have suggested that they are to be dated to the reconstruction of Britain by Theodosius, after the catastrophes of 367. At Alderney, the central tower is missing, but the outer enclosure, with its small projecting towers at the rounded corners, is so similar that this post must surely be contemporary with the Yorkshire sites.

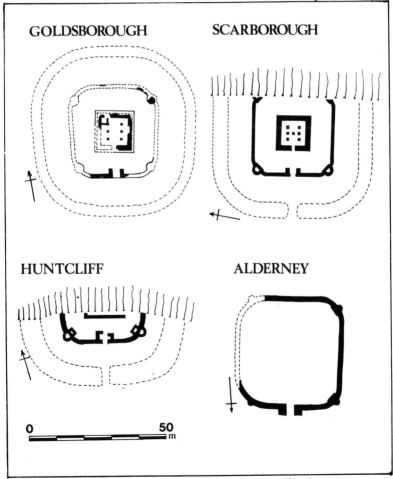

GOLDSBOROUGH

SCARBOROUGH

HUNTCLIFF

ALDERNEY

0   50
         m

Fig. 81 Comparative plans of signal stations (*burgi*) in
the north-east and in Alderney. Scale 1 : 1332.

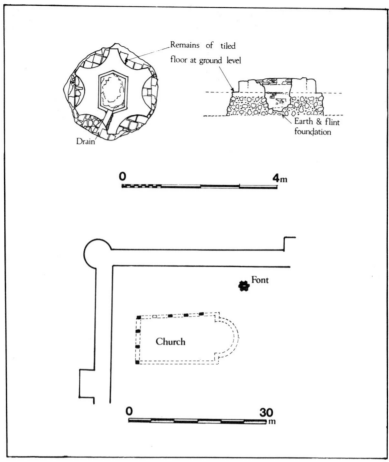

Fig. 82 The late Roman church and baptistery at
Richborough.

Of the British sites, only at Richborough is there any real evidence for a
continuation of use after 410. Here, finds of coins from the latest periods of
Roman rule in Britain outnumber other periods to a surprising degree, adding
archaeological substance to historical accounts of the continued use of the site
into the early years of the fifth century. In addition, one of the most unusual
interior buildings—a Christian church—has recently been recognized in the
north-west corner of the fort (Fig. 82).[28] Although these remains were
completely missed by the excavators, from their plans and photographs it is
possible to see that there was a timber-built rectangular structure in this area,
its main timber uprights resting on large blocks of stone which were soon
cleared away in excavating the lower, earlier levels. The one portion of the
church which was found in excavation was the baptismal font—a small
hexagonal tiled basin lined with hard mortar. From parallel finds at sites in

Germany and Switzerland also inside Roman forts, but under present-day parish churches, this enigmatic structure has now been properly interpreted. As in many of the churches known from inside late Roman forts, the baptistery will have lain between the church and the fort wall in a separate room from the main body of the church. The date of the church's construction is uncertain, but at the earliest it must be dated late in the fourth century.

By 410, the British part of the Saxon Shore system must have broken down, and although garrisons of troops had no doubt been maintained in some of the forts, at others it is clear that there can have been no such continuity. At Portchester the archaeological evidence seems to show that a military presence cannot have been maintained after 369, and although there was some occupation after this date, it was probably only a civilian phase of occupation, or maybe again soldier-settlers (by now more settler than soldier), who occupied the site as a refuge against the troubles of the coastal area in the later years of the fourth century. There is some evidence that other places along the south coast may also have been used as refuges for a civilian population at the same time, though evidence for the actual refortification of former Iron Age hill-forts cannot be tied down to a precise date in the fourth century. The hill-fort at Highdown and other hill-top sites along the southern coastline may have been thus used throughout this period. Highdown itself, in Sussex, has a Roman bath-house nearby, which is evidence of some permanence of occupation, possibly even by a regular garrison.

There is as yet no reliable evidence about the continuity of occupation by Saxons at former Roman sites on the Saxon Shore. Some of the forts—for example, Burgh Castle, Bradwell, Richborough, Dover, Pevensey and Portchester—have produced Saxon remains or figure in legends or historical sources of Saxon times. By 410, most of the forts must have been abandoned, at least for military purposes, and were perhaps used only by settlers or soldiers who had grown accustomed to the places, and stayed on inside the walls for protection. About the fifth century itself, particularly the first half, both archaeological evidence and historical sources are vague. The *adventus Saxonum*, the arrival of the Saxons, a historical event given particular importance by its mention in historical sources, has been placed at several dates in the early and mid fifth century. Saxon invasion, however, is unlikely to have been a single occurrence, but a long process which was no doubt promoted in some measure, albeit unwittingly, by the policies of such figures as Vortigern. This man appears to have held some kind of privileged position which is only explicable by supposing that in the years after 410 there was once again some support, however indirect, from the Roman government. He was possibly some sort of client governor over Britain, but his independence may have won him only the hostility of Rome, and fear of Rome's intervention resulted in his invitation to Saxons to settle near

Fig. 83 Antiquarian drawing of a pot of distinctively Saxon
style (possibly even 'Romano-Saxon') from the cemetery
at Burgh Castle. Scale 1:4.

Richborough and thus be ready to resist Roman reassertion of control.[29] This
episode, dated to 430 or thereabouts, marks the end of Roman influence over
Britain, though later, opponents of Vortigern, alarmed at the number of
Saxons arriving, were not above making an appeal for assistance to Aetius, the
magister militum in Gaul, in or around 446.

As for the forts of the Saxon Shore, there is evidence from the Anglo-Saxon
Chronicle that those of the south coast were pockets of local resistance to
Saxon arrivals; under the year 491, there is recorded a massacre of Britons at
Andreadsceaster (presumably the Roman *Anderida*) or Pevensey, and a few
years later, in 501, Port, a Saxon leader, landed at Portsmouth and won a
victory over a noble Briton.

The distinctive archaeological remains of the Anglo-Saxon period are the
cemeteries, and at Burgh Castle, in the field to the east of the fort, there lay not
only the Roman cemetery, but also an Anglo-Saxon urnfield cemetery.
Illustrations of urns found in the eighteenth century can be seen in antiquarian
publications (e.g. Fig. 83). There are no similar recent finds.

Later on, early Saxon Christian churches were established inside the walls
of at least three of the Saxon Shore forts (Fig. 84).[30] Burgh Castle is usually
claimed as the site of the monastery established in A.D. 630 by St Fursa at a
place that Bede, who recounts the event, calls 'Cnobheresburg'. In excavation
in 1958–61, fragmentary remains of plaster-work, possibly from the monastic
church, and the very faint outlines of oval huts, interpreted as the monastic
cells, were found. In addition, a cemetery containing over 150 bodies was

examined. This was certainly post or very late Roman in date, and must have been pre-Norman. It contained men, women and children, and could have been the cemetery of a community of Christians established within the fort, possibly of this Saxon monastic settlement. Another chapel was established at Bradwell by St Cedd. This still stands on the site of the west gate into the fort. At Reculver in 669, King Egbert of Kent granted the fort area to be the site of a monastery. Elsewhere there are other early traditions. St Augustine's

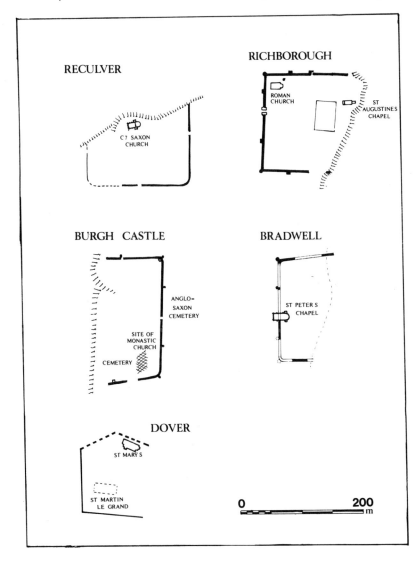

Fig. 84 The development of monasteries in Saxon Shore forts in the Saxon and later periods.

Chapel, the medieval remains of which can still be seen at Richborough (Fig. 84), was founded, so the story goes, to commemorate the site of the saint's landing in Britain on his way to see Ethelbert, King of Kent, in 597. It has also been suggested that the site granted by King Sigberht to St Felix for the foundation of his mission was not Dunwich, as is commonly supposed, following a 'late' tradition of British historical and antiquarian writers, but Walton Castle.[31] St Felix's mission, at *Dommoc*, and the Chapel of St Cedd at Bradwell are not likely to have been founded in sites which were deserted; Bradwell was a flourishing Saxon township, and Walton may have been likewise. Certainly Dunwich, if this is the correct identification of Felix's site, was a flourishing port in the later Saxon period.

Despite these foundations inside the forts, at none of the sites can there be said to be clear signs of continuity from late Roman to pagan or Christian Saxon periods. Even at Richborough, where the sites of both the late Roman church and the Saxon chapel are known, the two locations are quite different. At Portchester, too, there was a monastic establishment, but this seems to have followed a period inside the fort when the ground was in arable use after the Roman period. It is perhaps only at Dover (Fig. 84), where the present parish church of St Mary may still lie within the site of the Roman fort, that there is any chance of continuity in the use of a Christian site from the Roman period onwards. Under St Mary's (or part of it) lies a bath building, but it is also possible that there may have been a late Roman church inside the fort. The priory church of St Martin-le-Grand, which also lay inside the area of the fort, and may even have been aligned parallel with its south wall, is of uncertain date, but has a tradition which reaches back to Edbald in 616.

Thus ends the story of one of the most important frontiers of the later period of Rome's rule in the western empire. The system, once an answer so brilliant and successful to the Saxon raids of the late third century, adapted, modified and extended throughout the fourth, finally failed through lack of man-power by the early fifth and led to the breakdown of strategic defence on the empire's northern fringes. This exposed both British and Gallic coastlines to renewed Saxon attacks under which they finally succumbed.

It is worth recording how real was the terror instilled into Roman hearts at the mention of the Saxons, even as late as the fifth century. Sidonius, writing to his friend Rutilius on service in Gaul against Saxon marauders, distils the fear and horror which had earlier caused such an extensive system to be built up and maintained:

Please do be very careful—there's no time like the present for a warning. Saxons are the most brutal of enemies: they'll only attack if they have the advantage of surprise—if you see them first, they'll slink away. They avoid defended sites, but hit hardest at the unprepared. If they hunt, they'll catch, but if you pursue them, they'll escape . . . .[32]

NOTES

For bibliographical abbreviations, see p. 164

CHAPTER 1. THE SETTING

1. Schönberger, *JRS*, lix (1969), 177–8.
2. Aurelius Victor, *De Caesaribus*, XXXIII, 3; Eutropius, IX, 8.
3. Aurelius Victor, loc. cit.: 'Peoples of the Franks, causing havoc throughout Gaul, seized Spain. They sacked and virtually ruined the city of Tarragona, and then, getting hold of ships, a group of them even got as far as Africa.'
4. For an exaggerated, but contemporary summary of the benefits to the Roman state from the British provinces, see *Pan. Lat.*, VIII (V), 11.
5. Eutropius, IX, 21; Aurelius Victor, XXXIX, 20.
6. C. H. V. Sutherland, *Coinage and Currency in Roman Britain* (Oxford 1937), 156–8.
7. H. Koethe, 32 *Bericht der Römisch-Germanisch Kommission* (1942), 199–200. For coin-hoards in Spain, see A. Balil, *Cuadernos de Trabajos de la Escuela Española en Roma*, ix (1957), esp. 123f.
8. On the Roman view of such settlements, see *Pan. Lat.*, VIII (V), 21, 2.
9. B. Green and J. N. L. Myres, *The Anglo-Saxon Cemeteries of Caistor-by-Norwich and Markshall* (London 1973), 44–5, dating pottery of Saxon style found at Caistor to the later years of the third century.
10. White, *LS*, ch. 6.
11. On *laeti*-type metalwork from Britain, see S. C. Hawkes and G. C. Dunning, *Medieval Archaeology*, V (1961), 1f.; S. C. Hawkes, *Britannia*, v (1974), 386f. On the Continental metalwork, W. Böhme, *Germanische Grabfunde des 4 und 5 Jahrhunderts* (Münchener Beiträge zur Vor- und Frühgeschichte, 19, 1974).
12. Zosimus, I, 68—Burgundians and Vandals settled in Britain under Probus. Another often quoted reference is Ammianus Marcellinus, XXIX, 4, 7, where it might appear that Valentinian transferred a whole tribe of Bucinobantes to Britain. On this, and on *laeti* in Britain in general, see Frere, *Britannia*, 252 and 270 n. 5.
13. White, *LS*, 69f.
14. On this type of pottery, J. N. L. Myres in *Dark Age Britain*, Studies presented to E. T. Leeds, ed. D. B. Harden (London 1956), 16–39. See also J. N. L. Myres, *Anglo-Saxon Pottery and the Settlement of England* (Oxford 1969), 66f.
15. e.g. from Wijster, *Palaeohistoria*, XI, Fig. 104, 753, and Fig. 166, 1XB/3; see also examples from Continental sites in Böhme, op. cit., *passim*.
16. Sidonius Apollinaris, *Letters*, VIII, vi, 14f.
17. B. W. Cunliffe, *Richborough*, V, 255–6.
18. Frere, *Britannia*, 252 and 333.

19. S. E. Winbolt, *Roman Folkestone* (London 1925).

20. I. A. Richmond and O. G. S. Crawford, *Archaeologia*, XCIII (1949), 42.

21. C. B. Rüger, *Germania Inferior (Beihefte der Bonner Jahrbücher*, 30, 1968), 109f.; see also the finds from the various sites in *Der Niedergermanische Limes*, ed. J. Bogaers and C. B. Rüger (Kunst und Altertum am Rhein, 50, 1974).

22. W. A. Van Es, *De Romeinen in Nederland* (Bussum 1972), 96; W. Byvanck, *Excerpta Romana* II, 173–4.

23. Van Es, op. cit., 96; J. E. Bogaers, *Westerheem*, 23 (1974), 70f.

24. J. A. Trimpe Burger in *Deae Nehalenniae* (Leiden, Rijksmuseum van Oudheden, 1971), 44f.

25. W. J. Rodwell, 'Trinovantian towns and their setting; a case study' in W. J. Rodwell and T. Rowley, *The 'Small Towns' of Roman Britain*, *BAR*, 15 (1975), 93–4 and Fig. 5.

26. *CIL*, XII, 686.

27. I. A. Richmond, *Ant. J.*, xli (1961), 224f.; see also *JRS*, lv (1965), 220, and J. C. Mann, in CBA, 18, p. 15.

28. J. E. Ellison, *Norfolk Archaeology*, 1966, 60.

29. R. Dunnett, *Transactions of the Essex Archaeological Society* (3rd ser.), iii, pt. 1 (1971), 68–9.

30. I owe this suggestion to Mr S. E. Rigold.

31. B. Whitwell, *Roman Lincolnshire* (Lincoln 1970), 52.

32. J. S. Wacher, *Brough-on-Humber* (Leeds 1969), 25, 27.

33. SHA, *Vita Didii Juliani*, I, 7–9; see also Van Es, op. cit., 48, on the general state of raiding and piracy from the Chauci and the Chatti at this time.

34. Trier: E. M. Wightman, *Roman Trier and the Treveri* (London 1970), 92f. Tongres: J. Breuer, *La Belgique Romaine* (Brussels 1944), 67f.

35. Van Es, *BROB*, 15–16 (1965–6), 63f.; see also, on some of the sites abandoned at this period, Van Es, *ROB* paper no. 31 (=*Palaeohistoria*, XIV, 1968, 187f).

36. Jelgersma and van Regteren Altera, *ROB* paper no. 15 (1969).

37. J. S. Boersma, *BROB*, 17 (1967), 65f.

38. D. de Weerd, *BROB*, 18 (1968), 237f. I owe the latest information, in advance of publication, to Mr Trimpe Burger.

39. On all these possible military sites, see J. A. Trimpe Burger in *BROB*, 10–11 (1960–1), 195f., and in *Deae Nehalenniae*, op. cit., 44f.

40. C. Seillier, *Septentrion*, i (1970), 97f.

CHAPTER 2. CARAUSIUS

1. Aurelius Victor, XXXIX, 20.

2. Eutropius, IX, 21.

3. W. Seston, *Dioclétien et la Tetrarchie* (Paris 1946), p. 75.

4. White, *LS*, p. 24.

5. *Pan. Lat.*, VIII (V), 6.

6. *Pan. Lat.*, VIII (V), 12, 1.

7. *CIL*, VI, 1116.

8. *Pan. Lat.*, VIII (V), 12, 1.

9. Virgil, *Aeneid*, II. 282–3: *quibus Hector ab oris exspectate venis.*

10. Frere, *Britannia*, 350–2, giving the evidence for Roman schools in Britain and such slight evidence as there is among the merchant classes for familiarity with the Latin classics.

11. *Pan. Lat.*, X (II), 12.

12. *Pan. Lat.*, XI (III).

13. *Pan. Lat.*, VIII (V), 12, 2.

14. *Pan. Lat.*, VIII (V), 12, 1.

15. *Pan. Lat.*, VIII (V), 6, 1–2.

16. Eutropius, IX, 22; *Pan. Lat.*, VIII (V), 12, 2.

17. *Pan. Lat.*, VIII (V), 15, 1.

18. *Pan. Lat.*, VIII (V), 15, 2–16.

19. *Pan. Lat.*, VIII (V), 16, 2.

CHAPTER 4. THE *NOTITIA*

1. This is the view of Jones, *LRE*, Appendix II.

2. Text of this and all quotations from the *Notitia* comes from Seeck, *ND*.

3. As, for example, the Antonine Itinerary, or the Ravenna Cosmography.

4. Bede, *Historia Ecclesiae*, III, 22.

5. E. Ekwall, *English River-Names* (reprinted Oxford 1968), *s.v.* Adur.

6. So C. E. Stevens, *Arch. J.*, xcvii (1940), 137–8.

7. Frere, *Britannia*, 388.

8. *ND*, Occ. XL, 25. On the dating see Frere, *Britannia*, 262f.

9. But even these garrisons may not have been the original ones. A tile stamp of a different unit, the *Cohors I Aquitanica*, has now been found at Brancaster.

10. G. Boon, *Isca* (Cardiff 1972), 61f.

11. Frere, *Britannia*, 268.

12. *CIL*, XIII, 5190.

13. Ammianus Marcellinus, XXVI, 6, 12.

14. Ammianus Marcellinus, XXVII, 1, 2.

15. Stevens, op. cit., 137.

16. *ND*, Occ. XLI, 17; *Vicus Julius* is the modern Gemersheim.

17. *ND*, Occ. XLII, 23.

18. Zosimus, II, 51, 4.

19. *ND*, Occ. VII, 109.

20. *ND*, Occ. V, 76, 106, 255, and VII, 152.

21. Frere, *Britannia*, 268.

22. The chapters in the *Notitia* are Occ. XXXVII and XXXVIII.

23. But see S. E. Rigold, *JBAA*, xxiv (1961) 55f., arguing for Walton Castle as 'Dommoc', the site of the seventh-century monastery of St Felix, and thus having a Roman name similar to *Dommucium*.

24. Cunliffe in *Richborough*, V (1968), 270–1.

25. *ND*, Occ. V, 125–32. All the *Notitia* texts, however, have the word '*militum*'—troops—corrected by Seeck to '*limitum*'—frontiers, to correspond to the text in the following list of Duces.

CHAPTER 5. CONTINENTAL COMPARISON

1. *NGall*, III, 8.
2. *NGall*, III, 6.
3. *NGall*, II, 4 and 8.
4. *Pan. Lat.*, VIII (V), 6.
5. In addition, there exists a letter of Tiberius, written in Greek, dated A.D. 4, in which he says that he is at 'Bononia in Gaul', which may show that the name has some older origin.
6. Abbé Cornet, see chapter bibliography: White, *LS*, 58–9.
7. Ammianus Marcellinus, XV, 2, 3.

CHAPTER 6. THE DATE OF THE SYSTEM

1. On late Roman forts in general, H. von Petrikovits, *JRS*, lxi (1971), 178f.
2. Frere, *Britannia*, 379f.
3. C. F. C. Hawkes, *Arch. J.*, cvi (1949), 62f.
4. Record photographs taken by D. Atkinson during excavation at Caistor show the towers with the robbed wall behind them. On examination there appears to be nothing to show that the wall and towers are contemporary, as was originally supposed. The walls of Caistor have an external plinth at ground level, and the towers are built over the stepped face, just as at Burgh Castle.
5. S. S. Frere, *Antiquity*, xxiii (1949), 153f.
6. On another group of city walls, in *Gallia Belgica*, see J. S. Johnson, *Britannia*, iv (1973), 210f.
7. Though some of the towers at Dax in *Novempopulana* (south-western France) were added to the completed wall.
8. White, *LS*.
9. *Pan. Lat.*, VIII (V) 15, 5: *Cur portum classemque deseruit?*
10. For more detailed consideration of the dating of Richborough, see J. S. Johnson, *Britannia*, i (1970), 240f.
11. B. W. Cunliffe *et al.*, *Excavations at Portchester*, I, 422f.
12. *Pan. Lat.*, VIII (V).
13. *Pan. Lat.*, VIII (V).
14. The original interim publication of the section through the fort defences appeared in *Helinium*, ii (1962), 51f. More recently, the publication of the cemetery (*Archaeologia Belgica*, 135, 1971) has occasioned a provisional reassessment of the dating.
15. As later admired by Julian, *Convivium*, 314b.

CHAPTER 7. DEFENSIVE TACTICS

1. Victor, *De Caesaribus*, XXXIII, 3. On the raids into Spain and Africa see (most recently) J. M. Blazquez, *Hispania*, xxvii (1968), 3f.
2. For the evidence on wall-construction under Postumus, see van Gansbeke, *Latomus*, xiv (1955), 404. Sites where coins of Postumus are found in the wall-foundations were not necessarily built in his reign.

3. On Rome, see I. A. Richmond, *The City Wall of Imperial Rome* (Oxford 1930), an invaluable collection of the literary and archaeological evidence. Another early site is Dijon, reportedly built under Aurelian (Gregory of Tours, *Historia Francorum*, III, 19).

4. Ammianus Marcellinus, XVII, 6, where the Juthungi attempt to besiege towns *praeter solitum*—'against their usual practice'.

5. *FGH*, 101, fr. 5, where Eusebius, illustrating the surprising efficiency of the barbarian when dealing with Roman fortifications, tells how, during the reign of one of the Gallic usurpers (i.e. between 258 and 273), the walls of the city of the Tyrrhenians, a tribe of Lugdunensis, were besieged by Germans from across the Rhine. This must be a reference to Tours, the *Civitas Turonum*. But if Tours were really under siege at this time, the city walls (thought to date from the last quarter of the third century) were not yet built. It is possible that Eusebius has the date wrong.

6. *FGH*, IIa, 100, frs. 25, 27 and 29.

7. On Trier, E. M. Wightman, *Roman Trier and the Treveri* (London 1968), 98.

8. *Pan. Lat.*, VIII (V), 21, 2. It is possible that some of the damage at Autun was caused, not by barbarian raiding, but by a siege during the episode of the Gallic empire.

9. I. A. Richmond, 'The Romans in Redesdale' in *The History of Northumberland*, XV (Newcastle 1940), 97f. For representations on Trajan's Column of log platforms for *ballistae*, see C. Cichorius, *Die Reliefs der Traianssäule* (Berlin 1896 and 1900), 47, sc. lxvi (165–7).

10. E. W. Marsden, *Greek and Roman Artillery, Historical Development* (Oxford 1969), esp. 174f. On the ranges of Roman artillery, 91.

11. Richmond, op. cit., 67.

12. J. Morris, *PSIA*, xxiv (1948), 107.

13. Zürich, E. Vogt, *Der Lindenhof in Zürich* (Zürich 1948), 46f.; Wittnauer Horn, G. Bersu, *Das Wittnauer Horn* (Basel 1945), 37f.

14. The idea of enfilading a gate in this way had its origins further back in Augustan wall circuits of cities in the southern part of Gaul (as at Fréjus, Aix-en-Provence and Arles—see R.E.M. Wheeler, *JRS*, xvi (1926), 174f.). It was introduced to Britain in the use of massive double towers at city gateways—for example the Balkerne Gate at Colchester (M. R. Hull, *Roman Colchester*, 16f.) or at Verulamium (R. E. M. Wheeler, *Verulamium, a Belgic and two Roman cities*, 63f.).

15. Similar gates are found at Kellmünz and, slightly adapted, though the principle is the same, at Jünkerath. H. von Petrikovits, *JRS*, lxi (1971), 200.

16. Jones (*LRE*, III, 355–6) shows that many of the garrisons listed throughout the *Notitia* had been rearranged. Possibly therefore the stationing of the *Classis Anderetianorum* at Paris postdates the abandonment of Britain.

17. *ND*, Occ. XLII, 23.

18. On Caistor and Horncastle, M. Todd, *The Coritani* (London 1973), 42–3. On the possible sites off Skegness, J. B. Whitwell, *Roman Lincolnshire* (Lincoln 1970), 52–3.

19. B. W. Cunliffe, *Richborough*, V, 269.

20. White, *LS*, 39 and 60.

21. See, for example, the *Notitia Galliarum*, where Rouen, Aleth, Avranches, Coutances, Vannes and Nantes are listed as *civitates*.
22. White, *LS*, 60–1.
23. I. A. Richmond, *Proceedings of the Belfast Natural History Association*, 1928–9, 22–3.
24. A tile has been found in recent excavations, recording the presence of the *Cohors I Aquitanica*, possibly an earlier garrison than the *Equites Dalmatae* recorded in the *Notitia*.
25. G. Boon, *Isca* (Cardiff 1968).
26. White, *LS*, 52–3; C. E. Stevens, *Arch. J.*, xcvii (1940), 137f.
27. I. E. Moore, *PSIA*, xxiv (1948), 176. When the site at Corton was surveyed, remains of a building 25 yards (*c.* 23 m) square were recorded.
28. T. Johnson, *The London Archaeologist*, 2, 7 (1973–4), p. 163.
29. J. K. St Joseph, *JRS*, xliii (1953), 97.
30. On the Julian Alps frontier, see J. Sasel and others *Claustra Alpium Juliarum* (Ljubljana, 1971).
31. Cunliffe, *Richborough*, V, 262.
32. Eutropius, IX, 21.
33. Vegetius, *De Re Militari*, iv, 37.
34. *Pan. Lat.*, VIII (V), 12, 2.

CHAPTER 8. BREAKDOWN OF THE COMMAND

1. J. J. Wilkes, in *Britain and Rome*, ed. B. Dobson (Kendal 1966), 114f. That the northern frontier was affected between 296 and 305 is suggested by *Pan. Lat.*, VI (VII), 7, 1–2. See also Frere, *Britannia*, 383, and B. Dobson and D. J. Breeze, *Britannia*, iii (1972), 200f.
2. Construction under Constantius Chlorus was hinted at by C. E. Stevens, *Arch. J.*, xcvii (1940), 136.
3. C. H. V. Sutherland, *Coinage and Currency in Roman Britain* (Oxford, 1937), Appendix 3, 162f.
4. Eusebius, *Life of Constantine*, I, 25, 2, refers to a visit by Constantine to Britain.
5. A. Mocsy, in *Folia Archaeologica*, x (1958), 89f. In his article he claims that the commonly held Valentinianic date for all these posts is an over-simplification and that they could equally well belong to the Diocletianic or Constantinian period.
6. *ND*, Occ. XL, 22. Note also the presence of another unit of *barcarii* (a naval patrol) at Lancaster in the later period of occupation of the site. D. C. Shotter, *Britannia*, iv (1973), 206–9.
7. G. D. B. Jones, *The Carmarthen Antiquary*, vii (1971), 3–24, esp. 10–12. He notes not only the presence of a walled town at Carmarthen, but also other coastal sites which have produced some trace of later Roman material, such as Loughor and Pembroke itself.
8. Frere, *Britannia*, 396; Shotter, op. cit., 207; G. Webster, *The Roman Imperial Army* (London 1969), 158. The actual mosaic inscription is recorded in *CIL*, VII, 62.
9. Julius Firmius Maternus, *De Errore Profanarum Religionum*, XXXVIII, 6. The visit was made even though it was the depth of winter and the Channel crossing was

not regarded as safe. See also *Codex Theodosianus*, XI, 16, 5, and Ammianus Marcellinus, XX, 1, 1.

10. Ammianus Marcellinus, XX, 1, 1.

11. Ammianus Marcellinus, XXVI, 4, 5.

12. Ammianus Marcellinus, XXVII, 8.

13. R. Reece, *Britannia*, iv (1973), 227f. Note particularly Dr Reece's comments on p. 250 on the numbers of coins found as a proportion of about 0·1% of the total estimated to have been in circulation in the Roman period.

14. S. C. Hawkes and G. C. Dunning, *Medieval Archaeology*, v (1961), 1f. See also a supplementary note by Mrs Hawkes, *Britannia*, v (1974), 386f.

15. For example the fourth-century grave found at Richborough. This contained an inhumation burial with sword, spear and shield. See J. P. Bushe-Fox, *Richborough*, IV, 155.

16. As argued by J. Mertens in the introduction to his publication of the finds from the Oudenburg cemetery, *Archaeologia Belgica*, 135 (Brussels 1971), 36.

17. S. E. Rigold, in *Château Gaillard Studies*, III (1969), 128f.

18. See n. 10 above.

19. Ammianus Marcellinus, XXVIII, 3, 2.

20. R. Tomlin, *Britannia*, v (1974), 303f.

21. See the poems of Claudian written in honour of these campaigns: *De Consulatu Stilichonis*, ii, 250–5.

22. Nennius, *Historia Britonum*, 30; Zosimus, VI, 5.

23. D. Peacock, *Antiquity*, xlvii (1973), 138f.

24. White, *LS*, 63, though he uses the comparison to attempt to make the point that the sites on different sides of the Channel were built against different enemies.

25. In the *Notitia*, Occ. XXVII, his title is specifically *Comes Litoris Saxonici per Britannias*.

26. e.g. *ND*, Occ. XLII, 39–42 and 67, listing five units of *laeti* and *Sarmatae* settled or stationed at various points within *Belgica Secunda*.

27. On the relationship between these three commands in more detail, see S. Johnson, 'Coastal Commands in the *Notitia*', in P. Bartholomew and R. Goodburn (eds.), *Studies in the Notitia Dignitatum*, *BAR*, S15 (1976).

28. P. D. C. Brown, *Britannia*, ii (1971), 241f.

29. J. H. Ward, *Britannia*, iii (1972), 277f.

30. In more detail on this aspect of the use of the Saxon Shore forts, see S. E. Rigold, *Litus Romanum*, in CBA, 18, pp. 70f.

31. S. E. Rigold, *JBAA*, xxiv (1961), 55f., and xxxviii (1974), 97f.

32. Sidonius Apollinaris, *Letters*, VIII, 6, 14.

BIBLIOGRAPHY

(1) Contemporary and early historians:
Ammianus Marcellinus, ed. J. C. Rolfe (Loeb)
Bede, ed. C. Plummer (Oxford 1896)
Eutropius, ed. F. Ruehl (Teubner 1887)
Nennius, ed. F. Lot (Paris 1934)
Orosius, ed. C. Zangemeister (Leipzig 1889)
Panegyrici Latini, ed. R. A. B. Mynors (Oxford 1964) = *Pan. Lat.*
Sextus Aurelius Victor, ed. F. Pichlmayr (Teubner 1892)
Scriptores Historiae Augustae, ed. D. Magie (Loeb 1922–32) = *SHA*

(2) Periodicals

Ant. J.	*The Antiquaries Journal*
Arch. J.	*The Archaeological Journal*
Arch. Cant.	*Archaeologia Cantiana*
BROB	*Berichten van de Rijksdienst voor het Oudheidkundig Bodermonderzoek* (Reports of the Dutch State Archaeological Service)
JBAA	*Journal of the British Archaeological Association*
JRS	*Journal of Roman Studies*
PSIA	*Proceedings of the Suffolk Institute of Archaeology*
SAC	*Sussex Archaeological Collections*

(3) Other works and abbreviations

BAR	*British Archaeological Reports*
Blanchet	A. Blanchet, *Les Enceintes Romaines de la Gaule* (Paris 1907)
CBA, 18	Council for British Archaeology, Research Report 18 (1977) *The Saxon Shore*, ed. D. E. Johnston.
CIL	*Corpus Inscriptionum Latinarum*
Frere, *Britannia*	S. S. Frere, *Britannia, a history of Roman Britain* (2nd ed. London 1974)
FGH	F. Jacoby, *Die Fragmente der Greichischen Historiker* (Berlin and Leiden 1923–58)
ILS	*Inscriptiones Latinae Selectae*, ed. H. Dessau (Berlin 1892–1916, reprinted 1954–62)
Jones, *LRE*	A. H. M. Jones, *The Later Roman Empire*, I–III (Oxford 1964)
ND	*Notitia Dignitatum*, ed. O. Seeck (Berlin 1876)
NGall	*Notitia Galliarum*, ed. O. Seeck, with *ND* (Berlin 1876)
RCHM	*Royal Commission on Historical Monuments*
RIB	*The Roman Inscriptions of Britain*, I, ed. R. G. Collingwood and R. P. Wright (Oxford 1965)

VCH   *Victoria County History*
White, *LS*   D. A. White, *Litus Saxonicum* (Madison, Wisconsin, 1961)

CHAPTER 1. THE SETTING

For historical sources, see under the general bibliography (p. 162).

On the Germanic invasions and coin-hoards:
I. J. Manley, *The Effects of the Germanic Invasions into Gaul* (University of
   California, Publications in History, xvii, 2, 1934).
H. Koethe, 'Zur Geschichte Galliens in dritten Viertel des dritten Jahrhunderts',
   32 *Bericht der Römisch-Germanisch Kommission* (1942), 199f.
C. H. V. Sutherland, *Coinage and Currency in Roman Britain* (Oxford 1937), 154f.

On the British fleet:
D. Atkinson, '*Classis Britannica*' in *Historical Essays in Honour of James Tait* (1933),
   1f.
B. W. Cunliffe, 'The British fleet' in *Richborough*, V (1968).
Gerald Brodribb, 'Stamped tiles of the Classis Britannica', *SAC*, 107 (1969),
   102f.
C. Seillier and J-Y Gosselin, 'Nouvelles estampilles de la flotte de Bretagne . . .'
   Revue du Nord, 51 (1969), 363f.
H. Cleere, CBA, 18, 16f., and *Arch. J.*, cxxxi (1974), 171f.

British sites:
Caister-by-Yarmouth: J. A. Ellison, *Norfolk Archaeology*, XXIII (1962), 94f., and
   XXIV (1966), 45f.
Brough-on-Humber: J. S. Wacher, *Brough-on-Humber* (Leeds 1969).
Caistor-by-Norwich: C. F. C. Hawkes, *Arch. J.*, cvi (1949), 62f.
Rochester: A. C. Harrison, *Arch. Cant.*, lxxxv (1970), 95f., and lxxxvii (1972),
   121f.; A. C. Harrison and C. Flight, *Arch. Cant.*, lxxxiii (1968) 55f.

Continental sites:
C. Seillier, 'État de recherches sur le littoral, de la frontière Belge à la Somme',
   Septentrion, i (1970), 97f.
W. A. Van Es, *De Romeinen in Nederland* (Bussum 1972).
J. Bogaers and C. B. Rüger, *Der Niedergermanische Limes* (Kunst und Altertum
   am Rhein, 50, 1974).

CHAPTER 2. CARAUSIUS

In general, on the revolt of Carausius and Allectus:
Frere, *Britannia*, ch. 16.
White, *LS*, 19–32.
W. Seston, *Dioclétien et la Tetrarchie* (Paris 1946).
D. E. Eicholz, 'Constantius Chlorus' invasion of Britain', *JRS*, xliii (1953), 41f.
N. Shiel, 'The Episode of Carausius and Allectus', *BAR*, 40 (1977).
J. Casey, 'Carausius and Allectus—rulers in Gaul?', *Britannia*, viii (1977),
   283f.

Carausian coinage:

    P. H. Webb, in G. Mattingly and E. A. Sydenham, *Roman Imperial Coinage*, V, ii (1933).

    R. A. G. Carson, 'The mints and coinage of Carausius and Allectus', *JBAA*, xxii (1959), 33f., and 'The sequence marks on the coinage of Carausius and Allectus,' in *Mints, Dies and Currency*, Studies presented to A. Baldwin, 1971, 57f.

On the Arras medallion:

    A. J. Evans, *Numismatic Chronicle*, x (1930), 221f.

CHAPTER 3. THE BRITISH FORTS

Brancaster:

    J. K. St Joseph, *Ant. J.*, xvi (1936), 444f.
    F. Haverfield, *VCH, Norfolk*, I, 304f.
    J. L. Warner, *Proceedings of the Archaeological Institute*, 1847, 9f.

Burgh Castle:

    C. F. C. Hawkes and J. Morris, *Arch. J.*, cvi (1949), 68f.
    J. Morris, *PSIA*, xxiv (1948), 102f.
    JRS, li (1961), 183; lii (1962), 178.
    J. Ives, *Remarks on the Gariannonum of the Romans* (Yarmouth, 1803).
    J. J. Raven, *PSIA*, vi (1888), 345f.
    J. S. Johnson, *Burgh Castle* (HMSO Official Guide, 1978).

Walton Castle:

    C. Fox, *VCH, Suffolk*, I, 287 and 305.

Bradwell:

    RCHM, Essex, IV, *South-East* (London 1923), *s.v.* Bradwell, 13f.
    VCH, Essex, III, 52f.
    M. V. Taylor, *Transactions of the Essex Archaeological Society*, xvii (1926), 198f.
    J. J. Raven, *Trans. Essex Arch. Soc.*, vi (1898), 291f.
    Parker and Lewin, *Archaeologia*, XLI (1867), 439f.
    F. Chancellor, *Arch.J.*, xxxiv (1877), 212f.

Reculver:

    R. Jessup, *Antiquity*, X (1936), 179f.
    F. H. Thompson, *Arch. Cant.*, lxvi (1953).
    B. J. Philp, *Arch. Cant.*, lxxiii (1960), 96f.
    JRS, li (1961), 191; lii (1962), 190; liii (1963), 158; lvii (1967), 202; lviii (1968), 206.
    B. J. Philp, *The Roman Fort at Reculver* (1969).

Richborough:

    J. P. Bushe-Fox, *Richborough*, I (1926), II (1928), III (1932), IV (1949).
    B. W. Cunliffe (ed.), *Richborough*, V (1968).
    J. S. Johnson, *Britannia*, i (1970), 240f.

Dover:
R. E. M. Wheeler and C. J. Amos, *Arch. J.*, lxxxvi (1929), 47f.
S. E. Rigold, *Arch. J.*, cxxvi (1969), 78f.
B. J. Philp, *Kent Archaeological Review*, 1971, 69f.
B. J. Philp, *Roman Dover* (1973).
Britannia, ii (1971), 286; iii (1972), 351; iv (1973), 322; v (1974), 459; vi (1975), 283; vii (1976), 376; viii (1977), 424.

Lympne:
C. Roach Smith, *The Antiquities of Reculver, Richborough and Lympne*, (London 1850).
F. Haverfield, *VCH, Kent*, III, 55f.
JRS, xxxiv (1944), 85.
B. Cunliffe, CBA, 18, 29–30: *Britannia*, viii (1977), 425.

Pevensey:
S. E. Winbolt, *VCH, Sussex*, III, 5–6.
L. Salzman, *SAC*, 51 (1907), 99f., and 52 (1908), 83f.
J. P. Bushe-Fox, *JRS*, xxii (1932), 60f.
JRS, xxix (1939), 224.

Portchester:
B. W. Cunliffe, *Ant. J.*, xliii (1963), 218; xlvi (1966), 39f.; xlix (1969), 62f.; l (1970), 67f.; and lii (1972), 70f.; *Portchester*, I (Dorking 1975).

CHAPTER 4. THE *NOTITIA*

On the *Notitia Dignitatum* in general:
J. B. Bury, 'The *Notitia Dignitatum*', *JRS*, x (1920), 131f.
Jones, *LRE*, Appendix II.
F. S. Salisbury, 'The *Notitia Dignitatum* and the western mints', *JRS*, xxiii (1933), 217f., and 'On the date of the *Notitia Dignitatum*', *JRS*, xvii (1927), 102f.

On the British portions of the *Notitia*:
D. van Berchem, 'On some chapters of the *Notitia Dignitatum* relating to the defence of Gaul and Britain', *American Journal of Philology*, lxxvi (1955), 138f.
C. E. Stevens, 'The British sections of the *Notitia Dignitatum*', *Arch. J.*, xcvii (1940), 125f.
Frere, *Britannia*, ch. 11.
M. W. C. Hassall, CBA, 18, 7–10.

On the fort garrisons:
D. Hoffmann, *Das spätrömische Bewegungsheer und die Notitia Dignitatum*, (Epigraphische Studien, 7, 1969), *passim*.
White, *LS*, 45f.

On fort identifications:
B. W. Cunliffe, 'The British fleet', in B. W. Cunliffe (ed.) *Richborough*, V (1968), 255f.

S. E. Rigold, 'The supposed see of Dunwich', *JBAA*, xxiv (1961), 55f., and 'Further evidence about the site of "Dommoc"', *JBAA*, xxxviii (1974), 97f.

CHAPTER 5. CONTINENTAL COMPARISON

On the Continental sites in general:
White, *LS*, 56f.
J. Mertens, CBA, 18, 51f.

Nantes:
Blanchet, 56.
G. Durville, *Fouilles de l'Évêché de Nantes*, 1910–1913 (Supp. to *Bulletin de la Société Historique et Archéologique de Nantes*, 1913).

Vannes:
Blanchet, 60.
J. de la Martinière, *Annales de Bretagne* (Mélanges Loth), 1927, 104f.

Brest:
Blanchet, 60.
Gallia, xxv (1967), 225.
R. Sanquer, CBA, 18, 45f.

Alderney:
T. D. Kendrick, *The Archaeology of the Channel Islands*, i (1928), 254–9.
D. E. Johnston, CBA, 18, 31f.

Aleth:
L. Langouet, *Archéologie*, March 1974, 46f.
L. Langouet, CBA, 18, 38f.

Rouen:
Blanchet, 33f.
Gallia, xxiii (1965), 272f.
81e Congrès National des Sociétés Savantes (Rouen 1956).

Boulogne:
E. Will, *Revue du Nord*, 42 (1960), 363f.
C. Seillier, CBA, 18, 35f.

Oudenburg:
J. Mertens, *Helinium*, ii (1962), 51f.; *Archaeologia Belgica*, 135 (1971); Oudenburg, Romeinse Legerbasis aan de Noordzeekust, *Archaeologicum Belgii Speculum*, iv (1972).
J. Mertens, CBA, 18, 51f; *Archaeologica Belgica*, 206 (1978), 73f.

Brittenburg:
H. Dijkstra and F. C. Ketelaar, *Brittenburg, Raadsels rond een verdronken Ruine* (1965).

On the location of Continental sites:

E. Desjardins, *Géographie de la Gaule Romaine*, I (1876), 175f.
Abbé Cornet, *Annales du Cercle Archéologique de Mons*, 60 (1947).
K. Miller, *Die Peutingerische Tafel* (Stuttgart 1916).

CHAPTER 6. THE DATE OF THE SYSTEM

On late Roman forts in general:

H. Schönberger, 'The Roman frontier in Germany: an archaeological survey',
JRS, lix (1969), 144f., esp. 177f.
H. von Petrikovits, 'Fortifications in the north-western Roman empire from the
third to the fifth centuries A.D.', *JRS*, lxi (1971), 178f.
E. Anthes, 'Spätrömische Kastelle und feste Städte im Rhein- und Donaugebeit',
10 *Bericht der Römisch-Germanisch Kommission* (1917), 86f.

On Gallic city walls:

Blanchet, *passim*.
R. M. Butler, 'Late Roman town walls in Gaul', *Arch. J.*, cxvi (1959), 25f.
J. S. Johnson, 'A group of late Roman city walls in Gaul', *Britannia*, iv (1973),
210f.

Canterbury:

S. S. Frere, *Antiquity*, xxiii (1949), 153f.

CHAPTER 7. DEFENSIVE TACTICS

Late Roman artillery:

E. W. Marsden, *Greek and Roman Artillery, Historical Development* (Oxford 1969),
174f.

Tower and gate types:

R. Schültze, *Bonner Jahrbücher*, 118 (1909), 280f.

CHAPTER 8. BREAKDOWN OF THE COMMAND

On this period in general:

Frere, *Britannia*, chs. 16 and 17.
R. MacMullen, *Soldier and Civilian in the later Roman Empire* (Cambridge, Mass.,
1963).

Individual sites:

Forts in Wales: M. G. Jarrett, *The Roman Frontier in Wales* (Cardiff 1968).
Cardiff: J. Ward, *Archaeologia*, LVII (1899–1901), 335f.
Lancaster: G. D. B. Jones, *Arch. J.*, cxxvii (1970), 288f.; I. A. Richmond,
Transactions of the Lancashire and Cheshire Architectural and Historical Society,
105 (1953), 1f.
Chester: F. H. Thompson, *Roman Cheshire* (Chester 1965).
Carmarthen: G. D. B. Jones, *The Carmarthen Antiquary*, vii (1971), 3f.

Caistor: P. Rahtz, *Ant. J.*, xl (1960), 175f.

Horncastle: C. F. C. Hawkes, *Arch. J.*, ciii (1946), 22f.

Bitterne: P. W. Gathercole and M. A. Cotton, *Excavations at Clausentum* (London 1958).

On the coastal defences in western Britain:

Anne Dornier, *Roman Frontier Studies* (Tel Aviv 1967), 15f.

INDEX